The Master Key System Summarized

Summary of the Teachings of Dr. Charles Haanel with Summary Teachings of Prof. Wallace Wattles.

Edited By: George S. Mentz, JD, MBA, CWM

Master Key System Summarized and Decoded – G. Mentz, JD, MBA

Printed in the United States of America

ISBN 9780615159881

ID: 1093515
www.lulu.com

978-0-6151-5988-1   (90000)

For more information, tools, free books and other information see:
www.mastersofthesecrets.com
www.secretdecoded.com

Table of Contents

MODULE ONE

It is my privilege to enclose herewith Module One of this Guide. Would you bring into your life more power? Then, Get the power consciousness. Do you want More health? Then, Get the health consciousness. More happiness? Get the happiness consciousness.

Live the spirit of these things (health, wealth and happiness consciousness) until they become yours by right. It will become impossible to keep them from you. The things of the world are fluid to a power within man by which he rules them. You need not acquire this power. You already have it. But you do want to understand it; you want to use it; you want to control it; you want to impregnate yourself with it, so that you can go forward and carry the world before you.

Day by day, as you go on and on, as you gain momentum, as your inspiration deepens, as your plans crystallize through (desire, writing, visualizing, directing your emotions, and concentration), as you gain understanding, you will come to realize that this world is no dead pile of stones and timber, but that it is a living abundant thing! It is made up of the beating hearts of humanity and incredible supply. It is a thing of life and beauty and prosperity.

It is evident that it requires understanding to work with the globe's abundant material of this description. But those who come into this understanding are inspired by a new life -- a new force. They gain confidence and greater power each day. They realize their hopes, and their dreams come true. Life has a deeper, fuller, clearer meaning than before. All should have a richer and fuller life, and you must take steps to grow.

Harmony in the World Within will be reflected in the World Without by harmonious conditions, agreeable surroundings, the best of everything. It is the foundation of health and a necessary essential to all greatness, all power, all attainment, all achievement, and all success. Harmony in the World Within means the ability to control our thoughts and to determine for ourselves how any experience is to affect us. Harmony in the World Within results in optimism and affluence. Affluence Within results in Affluence Without. One can achieve peace through a harmonious relationship with the universe, people, and surroundings. This can begin with realizing the truth of the goodness and abundance of the world. This can be done through blessing, praising, and thanking the universe for all you have including health, talent, abilities, and events. Developing a harmonious gratitude and projecting it to the world will allow and force the world to cooperate with you.

MODULE TWO

Our difficulties are largely due to confused ideas and ignorance of our true interests. The great task is to discover the laws of nature to which we are to adjust ourselves. Clear thinking and moral insight are, therefore, of incalculable value. All processes, even those of thought, rest on solid foundations.

The keener the sensibilities, the more acute the judgment, the more delicate the taste, the more refined the moral feelings, the more subtle the intelligence, the loftier the aspiration -- the purer and more intense are the gratifications which existence yields. Hence, it is that, the study of the best that has been thought in the world, gives supreme pleasure.

The powers, uses, and possibilities of the mind under the new interpretations, are incomparably more wonderful than the most extravagant accomplishment, or even dreams of material progress. Thought is energy. Active thought is active energy; concentrated thought is concentrated energy.

Thought concentrated on a definite purpose becomes power. A definite purpose can be a goal, aspiration, or what you aim to be. This is the power which is being used by those who do not believe in the virtue of poverty, or the beauty of self-denial. They perceive that this is the talk of weaklings. You must rise above and begin to think that your thought controls your circumstances. If you whine and complain all day in your minds eye, then this will be attracted to you. Thus, it is imperative to give the attention of your mind to what is good, healthy, wealthy, and whole.

The ability to receive and manifest this power depends upon the ability to recognize the Infinite Energy ever dwelling in man, constantly creating and recreating his body and mind, and ready at any moment to manifest through him in any needful manner. In exact proportion to the recognition of this truth will be the manifestation in the outer life of the individual. Therefore, you shall begin to recognize the truth that all creation is part of you and the universe desires the best for you. By making this conclusion, you will form a connection to the spirit and universe. Your expectation of better things, your belief in your oneness with the world, and your beliefs will allow a new level of cooperation, energy, and force to enter your life.

MODULE THREE

You have found that the Individual may act on the Universal, and that the result of this action and interaction is cause and effect. Therefore, thought is the cause. And the experiences with which you meet in life are the effect.

Eliminate, therefore, any possible tendency to complain of conditions as they have been, or as they are, because it rests with you to change them and make them what you would like them to be. As stated, as within is without, and your character and being evolves according to what you think about all day long.

Direct your effort to a realization of the mental resources always at your command, from which all real and lasting power comes. Persist in this practice until you come to a realization of the fact that there can be no failure in the accomplishment of any proper object in life IF you but understand your power and persist in your object or goal. Because the mind-forces are ever ready to lend themselves to a purposeful will, in the effort to crystallize thought and desire into actions, events and conditions. Thus, your concentrated thought in one direction will force the whole of the world to begin sending solutions, answers, and assistance to you. As you will find later in the lessons, your concentrated desire, mixed with gratitude/harmony and vital emotions of love will begin all of this flow to you.

Whereas in the beginning of each function of life and each action is the result of conscious thought, the habitual actions become automatic and the thought that controls them passes into the realm of the subconscious; yet it is just as intelligent as before. It is necessary that it become automatic, or subconscious, in order that the self-conscious mind may attend to other things. The new actions will, however, in their turn, become habitual, then automatic, then subconscious in order that the mind again may be freed from this detail and advanced to still other activities. In this line of thought, at some point you will become very efficient at certain actions. Do to your proficiency, you will automatically begin to manifest from your intention and complete similar tasks and exercises with much greater ease. The Ancient Masons taught these principles, and you to can attain the light of this doctrine with practice.

When you realize this, you will have found a source of power, which will enable you to take care of any situation in life which may develop.

MODULE FOUR

Thought is energy and energy is power. It is because all the religions, sciences and philosophies with which the world has heretofore been familiar have been based upon the manifestation of this energy instead of the energy itself, that the world has been limited to effects, while causes have been ignored or misunderstood.

For this reason we have God and the Evil in religion, positive and negative in science, and good and bad in philosophy.

This philosophy reverses the process; it is interested only in cause, and the letters received from students tell a marvelous story. They indicate conclusively that students are finding the cause whereby they may secure for themselves health, harmony, abundance, and whatever else may be necessary for their welfare and happiness.

As such, if you have a toothache, you should not avoid a dentist when a simple filling may cure the pain or future damage. The same logic would hold that if you mentally or physically project resentment, anger, insults, poverty and other ills, that the thinking and action will attract to you these bad things.

Life is expressive and it is our business to express ourselves harmoniously and constructively. Sorrow, misery, unhappiness, disease and poverty are not necessities and we should be constantly eliminating them from our lives through constructive thought and action. But this process of eliminating consists in rising above and beyond limitation of any kind. He who has strengthened and purified his thought need not concern himself about arguments, criticism, and doubt, and he who has come into an understanding of the law of abundance will go at once to the source of the supply which is the supreme spirit of all.

It is thus, that fate, fortune, and destiny will be controlled as readily as a captain controls his ship, or an engineer, his train. The past is yesterday, the future is tomorrow, and today is now. Each day you must do all you can to prepare and better yourself through effective and efficient action.

MODULE FIVE

After reading this module carefully, you will see that every conceivable force or object or fact is the result of mind in action. Mind in action is thought, and thought is creative. Men are thinking now as they never thought before. Therefore, this is a creative age, and the world is awarding its richest prizes to the thinkers who take action under the prescribed science of desire, gratitude, harmony, love, and worthiness of receipt.

Matter is powerless, passive, inert. Mind is force, energy, power. Mind shapes and controls matter. Every form which matter takes is but the expression of some pre-existing thought. But thought works no magic transformations; it obeys natural laws; it sets in motion natural forces; it releases natural energies; it manifests in your conduct and actions, and these in turn react upon your friends and acquaintances, and eventually upon the whole of your environment.

You can originate thought, and, since thoughts are creative, you can create for yourself the things you desire if you are willing to harmoniously cooperate with the Universe, mentally believe on a specific level that you can have it, take action and allow yourself to receive the good by putting a foundation in place.

MODULE SIX

Module Six provides an excellent understanding of the most wonderful mechanism which has ever been created. A mechanism whereby you may create for yourself Health, Strength, Success, Prosperity or any other condition which you desire. Necessities are demands, and demands create action, and actions bring about results. The process of evolution is constantly building our tomorrows out of our todays. Individual development, like Universal development, must be gradual with an ever-increasing capacity and volume.

The knowledge that if we infringe upon the rights of others, we become moral thorns and find ourselves entangled at every turn of the road, should be an indication that success is contingent upon the highest moral ideal, which is "The greatest good to the greatest number."

Aspiration, desire, and harmonious relations, constantly and persistently maintained will accomplish results. The greatest hindrance is erroneous and fixed ideas. Go beyond your doubt and say, "Why Not". Don't let the nay Sayers convince you that you may fail. Don't even talk to them. Only speak with experts and those who have excelled. Speak with those who are supportive and encouraging. Moreover, you may have convinced yourself that certain things are doomed to fail, but ALWAYS try to see beyond what is apparent, seek more, and discover solutions that others have failed to see.

To be in tune with eternal truth we must possess poise and harmony within. In order to receive intelligence, the receiver must be in tune with the transmitter. One can achieve this harmony through gratitude. Gratitude creates an expectation of better things if practiced daily. Gratitude brings you closer to the Universe and Spirit Energy. Your connection will be reinforced and renewed. Additionally, Gratitude, Praise, and Thanks to the world on a frequent basis dispels doubt, dissatisfaction, and other mental blocks. Overall, thanks and gratitude create faith and expectation of the BEST instead of always being some type of realist who demands that bad things MUST happen so they can be correct with their theories of negativity.

Thought is a product of Mind, and Mind is creative. But this does not mean that the Universal will change its modus operandi (mission) to suit us or our ideas. It does mean that we can come into harmonious relationship with the Universal, and when we have accomplished this we may ask anything to which we are entitled, and the way will be made plain.

Action is required. People must be contacted. Doors must be knocked upon. Requests must be made. Other people are here from the spirit also. Many are placed in front of you to HELP you. If you do not ask, then the universe has done its job until you do. As the Jesuit Catholic Mystics professed, a man who is contemplative in action is powerful indeed.

MODULE SEVEN

Through all the ages man has believed in an invisible power, through which and by which all things have been created and are continually being re-created.

We may personalize this power and call it God, or we may think of it as the essence or spirit, which permeates all things, but in either case the effect is the same. So far as the individual is concerned, the objective, the physical, the visible, is the personal, that which can be known by the senses. It consists of body, brain and nerves. The subjective is the spiritual, the invisible, the impersonal.

The personal is conscious because it is a personal entity. The impersonal, being, is not conscious of itself and has therefore been termed the subconscious. The personal, or conscious, has the power of will and choice, and can therefore exercise discrimination in the selection of methods whereby to bring about the solution of difficulties. The impersonal, or spiritual, being a part or one with the source, and origin of all power, can necessarily exercise no such choice, but, on the contrary, it has Infinite resources at its command. It can and does bring about results by methods concerning which the human or individual mind can have no possible conception.

You will therefore see that it is your privilege to depend upon the human will with all its limitations and misconceptions, or you may utilize the potentialities of Infinity by making use of the subconscious mind. Here, then, is the scientific explanation of the wonderful power, which has been put within your control, if you but understand, appreciate and recognize it.

With the conscious and sub-conscious being addressed, we can impress upon our minds truths and possibilities through the process of auto-suggestion, mental imagery, and conditioning.

Some of the greatest success stories and philosophers have used the technique of writing out positive and declarative statements to be read on a daily basis. The use of collages and pictures can also be used. By reading these statements and concentrating on pictures, we can impress our conscious, sub-conscious and spiritual levels. Example: "I am getting better and better each day" This statement read silently or out loud each day for a month would change the way you think on a cognizant level and on a spiritual level within. Moreover, the images of a beautiful home that you would like taped to your wall would impress your mind on several levels to cooperate and help you attain this home over time.

MODULE EIGHT

In Module Eight, you will find that you may freely choose what you think, but the result of your thought is governed by a never changing law! Is not this a wonderful thought? Is it not wonderful to know that our lives are not subject to sudden change or variability of any kind? That they are governed by law. This stability is our opportunity, because by complying with the law we can secure the desired effect with invariable precision.

It is the Law which makes the Universe one grand SONG of Harmony. If it were not for law, the Universe would be a Chaos instead of a Cosmos. Here, then, is the secret of the origin of both good and evil, this is all the good and evil there ever was or ever will be. Let me illustrate. Thought results in action. If your thought is constructive and harmonious, the result will be good. If your thought is inharmonious, the result will be destructive to your success.

There is therefore but one law, one principle, one cause, one Source of Power. Good and evil are simply words which have been coined to indicate the result of our action, or our compliance or non-compliance with this law.

The importance of this is well illustrated in the lives of *Emerson and **Carlyle. Emerson loved the good and his life was a symphony of peace and harmony. Carlyle hated the bad, and his life was a record of perpetual discord and dis-harmony.

Here we have two grand men, each intent upon achieving the same ideal, but one makes use of constructive thought and is therefore in harmony with Natural Law, the other makes use of destructive thought and therefore brings upon himself discord of every kind and character.

It is evident therefore that we are to hate nothing -- not even the "bad, " -- because hatred is destructive, and we shall soon find that by entertaining destructive thought we are sowing the "wind" and in turn shall reap the "whirlwind."

With this rule in mind, you should understand that disharmony, hate, and resentment are VERY VERY distracting from your purpose and mental energies. Realize that a pure mind of gratitude, harmony, and confident expectation are very efficient. A pure mind can focus on REAL goals and aspirations in a VERY effective way. In addition, your harmonious mind has the ability to take very constructive action on a daily basis without worry, fear, and hatred looming in the back of it.

MODULE NINE

In Module Nine, you may learn to fashion the tools by which you may build for yourself any condition you desire. If you wish to change conditions you must change yourself. Your whims, your wishes, your fancies, your ambitions may be thwarted at every step, but your inmost thoughts will find expression just as certainly as the plant springs from the seed.

Suppose, then, we desire to change conditions, how are we to bring this about? The reply is simple: By the law of growth. Cause and effect are as absolute and undeviating in the hidden realm of thought as in the world of material things.

Hold in mind the condition desired; <u>affirm it as an already existing fact</u>. This indicates the value of a powerful affirmation. By constant repetition it becomes a part of ourselves. We are actually changing ourselves; are making ourselves what we want to be.

<u>Character is not a thing of chance, but it is the result of continued effort</u>. If you are timid, vacillating, self-conscious, or if you are over-anxious or harassed by thoughts of fear or impending danger, remember that is axiomatic that "two things cannot exist in the same place at the same time." Exactly the same thing is true in the mental and spiritual world; so that your remedy is plainly to substitute thoughts of courage, power, self-reliance and confidence, for those of fear, lack and limitation.

The easiest and most natural way to do this is to select a verbal or mental affirmation which seems to fit your particular case. The positive thought will destroy the negative as certainly as light destroys darkness, and the results will be just as effectual. Act is the blossom of thought, and conditions are the result of action, so that you constantly have in your possession the tools by which you will certainly and inevitably make or unmake yourself, and joy or suffering will be the reward.

We can make no mistake about this if we realize that truth is the vital principle of the Universal Mind and is Omnipresent. For instance, if you require health, a realization of the fact that the "I" in you is spiritual and that all spirit is one; that wherever a part is; the whole must be, will bring about a condition of health, because every cell in the body must manifest the truth as you see it. If you see perfection and wholeness, they must manifest perfection and wholeness in your life. The affirmation, "I am whole, perfect, strong, powerful, loving, harmonious and happy", will bring about harmonious conditions.

The reason for this is because the affirmation is in strict accordance with the Truth, and when truth appears every form of error or discord must necessarily disappear.

MODULE TEN

If you get a thorough understanding of Module Ten, you will have learned that nothing happens without a definite cause. You will be enabled to formulate your plans in accordance with exact knowledge. You will know how to control any situation by bringing adequate causes into play. When you win, as you will, you will know exactly why.

The ordinary man, who has no definite knowledge of cause and effect, is governed by his feelings or emotions. He thinks chiefly to justify his action. If he fails as a businessman, he says that luck is against him. If he dislikes music, he says that music is an expensive luxury. If he is a poor office man, he says that he could succeed better at some outdoor work. If he lacks friends, he says his individuality is too fine to be appreciated.

He never thinks his problem through to the end. In short, he does not know that every effect is the result of a certain definite cause, but he seeks to console himself with explanations and excuses. He thinks only in self-defense.

On the contrary, the man who understands that there is no effect without an adequate cause thinks impersonally. He gets down to facts regardless of consequences. He is free to follow the trail of truth wherever it may lead. He sees the issue clear to the end, and he meets the requirements fully and fairly, and the result is that the world gives him all that it has to give, in friendship, honor, love and approval. If your thought is in harmony with the creative Principle of Nature, it is in tune with the Infinite Mind, and it will form the circuit, it will not return to you void; but it is possible for you to think thoughts that are not in tune with the Infinite, and when there is no polarity, the circuit is not formed. What, then, is the result?

What is the result when a dynamo is generating electricity, the circuit is cut off and there is no outlet? The dynamo stops. Therefore, it is imperative that you form a constructive relationship with the infinite.

Learn to praise and you will be praised. If you give respect, you will receive it. If you provide opportunity, you will be afforded opportunity. If you give of yourself to help others, you will be helped. If you take action toward a goal every day, your goal will come to you. When you risk giving love unconditionally, you will be loved in return by the correct people. And, the law demands that when you draw closer to the spirit of harmony, the universal good of the world will meet you half way and come towards you with peace and abundance.

MODULE ELEVEN

Our life is governed by law - by actual, immutable principles that never vary. Law is in operation at all times; in all places. Fixed laws underlie all human actions. For this reason, those who control giant industries are enabled to determine with absolute precision just what percentage of every hundred thousand people will respond to any given set of conditions.

It is well, however, to remember that while every effect is the result of a cause, <u>the effect in turn becomes a cause</u>, which creates other effects, which in turn create still other causes; so that when you put the law of attraction into operation you must remember that you are starting a train of causation for good or otherwise which may have endless possibilities. This is much like any legal principle of causation where one action or omission can provide the domino affect.

We frequently hear it said, "A very distressing situation came into my life, which could not have been the result of my thought, as I certainly never entertained any thought which could have such a result."

We fail to remember that like attracts like in the mental world, and that the thought which we entertain brings to us certain friendships, companionships of a particular kind, and these in turn bring about conditions and environment, which in turn are responsible for the conditions of which we complain. The truth must be told to each generation and to every people in new and different terms, so that when the Great Teacher said -- "Believe that ye receive and ye shall receive" or, when Paul said -- "Faith is the substance of things hoped for, the evidence of things not seen" or, when modern science says -- "The law of attraction is the law by which thought correlates with its object", each statement when subjected to analysis, is found to contain exactly the same truth. The only difference being in the form of presentation.   As such, people who complain and resist good attract negative circumstances in their lives. Thoughts are things and substance. Your thought can create probabilities. Constructive thought in conjunction with gratitude, visualization, action, and knowing can increase probabilities of good, well being, and opportunity.

For your exercise in this Module, concentrate on the quotation taken from the Bible, "Whatsoever things ye desire, when ye pray, believe that ye receive them and ye shall have them"; [Mark 11:24] notice that there is no limitation, "Whatsoever things" is very definite and implies that the only limitation which is placed upon us in our ability to think, to be equal to the occasion, to rise to the emergency, to remember that Faith is not a shadow, but a substance, "the substance of things hoped for, the evidence of things not seen." [Hebrews 11:1]

Philippians IV

4 Rejoice in the Lord always. Again I will say, rejoice! 5 Let your gentleness be known to all men. The Lord [is] at hand. 6 Be anxious for nothing, but in everything by prayer and supplication, with thanksgiving, let your requests be made known to God; 7 and the peace of God, which surpasses all understanding, will guard your hearts and minds through Christ Jesus. 8 Finally, brethren, whatever things are true, whatever things [are] noble, whatever things [are] just, whatever things [are] pure, whatever things [are] lovely, whatever things [are] of good report, if [there is] any virtue and if [there is] anything praiseworthy -- meditate on these things. 9 The things which you learned and received and heard and saw in me, these do, and the God of peace will be with you. 10 But I rejoiced in the Lord greatly that now at last your care for me has flourished again; though you surely did care, but you lacked opportunity. 11 Not that I speak in regard to need, for I have learned in whatever state I am, to be content: 12 I know how to be abased, and I know how to abound. Everywhere and in all things I have learned both to be full and to be hungry, both to abound and to suffer need. 13 I can do all things through Christ who strengthens me.

Read the above and think about: gentleness, thanksgiving, constructive petitions, request for blessings, meditating on noble and optimistic thoughts, rejoicing in life, and even blessing yourself and your future......

MODULE TWELVE

"You must first have the knowledge of your power; second, the courage to dare; third, the faith to do."

If you concentrate upon the thoughts given, if you give them your entire attention, you will find a world of meaning in each sentence, and will attract to yourself other thoughts in harmony with them, and you will soon grasp the full significance of the vital knowledge upon which you are concentrating.

Knowledge does not apply itself; we as individuals must make the application, and the application consists in fertilizing the thought with a living purpose.

The time and thought which most persons waste in aimless effort would accomplish wonders if properly directed with some special object in view. In order to do this, it is necessary to center your mental force upon a specific thought and hold it there, to the exclusion of all other thoughts. If you have ever looked through the viewfinder on any camera, you may find that when the object was not in focus, the impression was indistinct and possibly blurred, but when the proper focus was obtained the picture was clear and distinct. This illustrates the power of concentration. Unless you can concentrate upon the object, which you have in view, you will have but a hazy, indifferent, vague, indistinct and blurred outline of your ideal and the results will be in accordance with your mental picture.

Keep in mind that you can be creative or competitive. However, there is no need to compete when you can provide a new and innovative product, service, or other. There is plenty to go around and new ideas help people to become more effective, live life better, and improve the world.

Overall, creating a specific and measurable goal or ideal of what you desire, can allow you to devote your attention to bringing it about. I am sure you have seen somebody who loves his or her work. They do their craft without interruption and with intense focus. They finish one task at a time, and they do it RIGHT the first time. You cannot worry about doing it wrongly; you must do it until you become a skillful master at a task.

Engaging action with boldness and single-mindedness of purpose will result in efficient exercises and tasks. In general, if you are a creative person, you may seek through trial and error to engage a task effectively. In any event, your pointed efforts can lead to great discoveries and innovations.

> *Then, indecision brings its own delays,*
> *And days are lost lamenting over lost days.*
> *Are you in earnest? Seize this very minute;*
> *What you can do, or dream you can do, begin it;*
> *Boldness has genius, power and magic in it.*

Johann Wolfgang von Goethe

MODULE THIRTEEN

Physical science is responsible for the marvelous age of invention in which we are now living, but spiritual science is now setting out on a career whose possibilities no one can foretell. Spiritual science has previously been the football of the uneducated, the superstitious, the mystical, but people are now interested in definite methods and demonstrated facts only. We have come to know that thinking is a spiritual process, that vision and imagination preceded action and event, that the day of the dreamer has come. The following lines by Mr. Herbert Kaufman are interesting in this connection.

"They are the architects of greatness, their vision lies within their souls, they peer beyond the veils and mists of doubt and pierce the walls of unborn Time. The computer operating system, wireless communications, the medical cures are bigger than life. Makers of Empires, they have fought for bigger things than crowns, and higher seats than thrones. Your homes are set upon the land a dreamer found. The pictures on its walls are visions from a dreamer's soul. They are the chosen few -- the blazers of the way. Walls crumble and Empires fall, the tidal wave sweeps from the sea and tears a fortress from its rocks. The rotting nations drop off from Time's bough, and only things the dreamer's make, live on."

Have you every wondered why the dreams of the dreamer come true. People use the Law Of Causation by which dreamers, inventors, authors, financiers, bring about the realization of their desires. The thing pictured upon our mind eventually becomes our own.

Each student should focus on these steps in this module:

1. What are your desires?
2. Can you envision achieving them?
3. Do you have the ability to select a definite goal and purpose to complete?
4. Are you willing to engage a harmonious relationship with the world and universe?
5. Are you willing to take action?
6. Are you willing to focus and concentrate on nothing else all day every day?
7. Can you affirm to yourself verbally and with mental images the successful completion of your desires?
8. Is it possible for you to believe that you have possession of your desires NOW and IN THIS MOMENT as if you actually HAVE them...?
9. Can you live, speak and act in a constructive way in which your words, thoughts and actions are in concordance with prosperity, abundance, and peace?

MODULE FOURTEEN

You have found from your study thus far that thought is a spiritual activity and is therefore endowed with creative power. This does not mean that some thought is creative, but that all thought is creative. This same principle can be brought into operation in a negative way, through the process of denial.

The conscious and subconscious are but two phases of action in connection with one mind. The relation of the subconscious to the conscious is quite analogous to that existing between a weather vane and the atmosphere. Just as the least pressure of the atmosphere causes an action on the part of the weather vane, so does the least thought entertained by the conscious mind produce within your subconscious mind action in exact proportion to the depth of feeling characterizing the thought and the intensity with which the thought is indulged.

It follows that if you deny unsatisfactory conditions, you are withdrawing the creative power of your thought from these conditions. You are cutting them away at the root. You are sapping their vitality.   As the old parable goes, we must take preemptive strikes to prevent the weeds of dissent and destruction from growing in our minds of great possibilities.

Remember that the law of growth necessarily governs every manifestation in the objective, so that a denial of unsatisfactory conditions will not bring about instant change. A plant will remain visible for some time after its roots have been cut, but it will gradually fade away and eventually disappear, so the withdrawal of your thought from the contemplation of unsatisfactory conditions will gradually, but surely, terminate these conditions.

You will see that this is an exactly opposite course from the one which we would naturally be inclined to adopt. It will therefore have an exactly opposite effect to the one usually secured. Most persons concentrate intently upon unsatisfactory conditions, thereby giving the condition that measure of energy and vitality which is necessary in order to supply a vigorous growth.   In conclusion, realists predict that misery is guaranteed. Would you not prefer to be the advocate of the spirit of all possibilities instead of a "Doubting Thomas" who seems methodically justified in playing the Devil's advocate. It is your choice.

And, the open-minded soul can achieve greatness through rejecting abject negativity and going to a higher level of consciousness....

MODULE FIFTEEN

Experiments with parasites found on plants indicate that even the lowest order of life is enabled to take advantage of natural law. This experiment was made by Jacques Loch, M.D., Ph. D., a distinguished member of the Rockefeller Institute.

"In order to obtain the material, potted rose bushes are brought into a room and placed in front of a closed window. If the plants are allowed to dry out, the aphids (parasites), previously wingless, change to winged insects. After the metamorphosis, the animals leave the plants, fly to the window and then creep upward on the glass."

It is evident that these tiny insects found that the plants on which they had been thriving were dead, and that they could therefore secure nothing more to eat and drink from this source. The only method by which they could save themselves from starvation was to grow temporary wings and fly, which they did.

Experiments such as these indicate that Omniscience as well as Omnipotence is omnipresent and that the tiniest living thing can take advantage of it in an emergency.

Part Fifteen tells you more about the law under which we live. It will explain that these laws operate to our advantage; that all conditions and experiences that come to us are for our benefit; that we gain strength in proportion to the effort expended, and that our happiness is best attained through a conscious cooperation with natural laws. In the physical world there is a law of compensation which is that "the appearance of a given amount of energy anywhere means the return or disappearance of the same amount somewhere else," and so we find that we can get only what we give; if we pledge ourselves to a certain action we must be prepared to assume the responsibility for the development of that action.

The subconscious cannot reason. It takes us at our word; we have asked for something; we are now to receive it; we have made our bed, we are now to lie in it; the die has been cast; the threads will carry out the pattern we have made.

At this juncture, we can only prepare to receive the good that the universe desires to send us. We must set into motion and create the necessary receptacles for effective receipt of prosperity. Example: You cannot receive a phone call without a phone, money wire without a bank account, and email without the internet...

MODULE SIXTEEN

The vibratory activities of the planetary Universe are governed by a law of periodicity. Everything that lives has periods of birth, growth, fruition, and decline. These periods are governed by the Septimal Law or Law of 7's.

The Law of Sevens governs the days of the week, the phases of the moon, the harmonies of sound, light, heat, electricity, magnetism, atomic structure. It governs the life of individuals and of nations, and it dominates the activities of the commercial world.

Life is growth, and growth is change, each seven years period takes us into a new cycle. The first seven years is the period of infancy. The next seven the period of childhood, representing the beginning of individual responsibility. The next seven represents the period of adolescence. The fourth period marks the attainment of full growth. The fifth period is the constructive period, when men begin to acquire property, possessions, a home and family. The next from 35 to 42, is a period of reactions and changes, and this in turn is followed by a period of reconstruction, adjustment and recuperation, so as to be ready for a new cycle of sevens, beginning with the fiftieth year. (For more information on the Laws of Sevens, please investigate the ancient Rosicrucian doctrines).

There are many who think that the world is just about to pass out of the sixth period; that it will soon enter into the seventh period, the period of readjustment, reconstruction and harmony; the period which is frequently referred to as the New Millennium.

Those familiar with these cycles will not be disturbed when things seem to go wrong, but can apply the principle outlined in these lessons with the full assurance that a higher law will invariably control all other laws, and that through an understanding and conscious operation of spiritual laws, we can convert every seeming difficulty into a blessing. The power to create depends entirely upon spiritual power; there are <u>three steps, idealization (selecting an ideal outcome or goal), visualization and materialization</u>. Every captain of industry depends upon this power exclusively.

It is by the exercise of this power that we take our fate out of the hands of chance, and consciously make for ourselves the experiences which we desire, because when we consciously <u>realize</u> a condition, that condition will eventually manifest in our lives; it is therefore evident that in the last analysis thinking is the one great cause in life.

The quality depends upon its substance, and this depends upon the material of which the mind is composed; if this material has been woven from thoughts of vigor, strength, courage, and determination, the thought will possess these qualities. And finally, the vitality depends upon the feeling with which the thought is impregnated. If the thought is constructive, it will possess vitality; it will have life, it will grow, develop, expand, it will be creative; it will attract to itself everything necessary for its complete development. To realize something means to have it in your heart, mind and emotions. Realization is knowing that you are worthy of good and expect the best.

If you wish to bring about the realization of any desire, form a mental picture of success in your mind, by consciously visualizing your desire; in this way you will be compelling success, you will be externalizing it in your life by scientific methods. Visualization must, of course, be directed by the will; we are to visualize <u>exactly</u> what we desire; we must be careful not to let the imagination run riot. Imagination is a good servant but a poor master, and unless it is controlled it may easily lead us into all kinds of speculations and conclusions which have no basis or foundation of fact whatever. Every kind of plausible opinion is liable to be accepted without any analytical examination and the inevitable result is mental chaos.

For your exercise in this Module, try to bring yourself to a realization of the important fact that harmony, peace, gratitude, and happiness are states of consciousness and do not depend upon the possession of things.   That things are effects and come as a consequence of correct mental states. So, if we desire material possession of any kind, our chief concern should be to acquire the mental attitude which will bring about the result desired. This mental attitude is brought about by a realization of our spiritual nature and our unity with the Universal Mind which is the substance of all things. This realization will bring about everything which is necessary for our complete enjoyment. This is scientific or correct thinking. When we succeed in bringing about this mental attitude it is comparatively easy to realize our desire as an <u>already accomplished fact</u>; when we can do this we shall have found the "Truth" which makes us "free" from every lack or limitation of any kind.

The key to this module is this fact, "Most people are not familiar with these principles during the fist few cycles of their lives."   If you develop a command of the information in this book, you can obtain an advanced standing and understanding of life along with being prepared for your opportunities and blessings.

MODULE SEVENTEEN

The student who masters this section will not mistake the symbols for the reality; he will be interested in causes, rather than effects. He will concentrate on the realities of life, and will then not be disappointed in the results.

All mental discovery and attainment are the result of desire plus concentration; desire is the strongest mode of action; the more persistent the desire, the more authoritative the revelation. Desire added to concentration will wrench any secret from nature. The intensity of one moment's earnest concentration and the intense longing to become and to attain may take you further than years of slow normal and forced effort; it will unfasten the prison bars of unbelief, weakness, impotence and self-belittlement, and you will come into a realization of the joy of overcoming.

If you wish to eliminate fear, concentrate on courage. If you wish to eliminate lack, concentrate on abundance. If you wish to eliminate disease, concentrate on health and gratitude for a perfect and harmonious body. Always concentrate on the ideal circumstances as already existing fact; this is the life principle which goes forth and sets in motion those causes which guide, direct and bring about the necessary relations, which eventually manifest in your life and mind.

See the source of your supply as a loving universe. Believe that all is possible with your partnership with the Supreme. Combine this emotion and feeling with your desires, concentration and ideals.

MODULE EIGHTEEN

In order to grow we must obtain what is necessary for our growth. This is brought about through the Law Of Attraction. This principle is the sole means by which the individual is differentiated from the Universal.

Think for a moment, what would a man be if he were not a husband, father, or brother, if he were not interested in the social, economical, political or religious world. He would be nothing but an abstract theoretical ego. He exists, therefore, only in his relation to the whole, in his relation to other human beings, in his relation to society. This relation constitutes his environment and harmonious interaction with the world.

It is evident, therefore, that the individual is simply a part of the one Universal Mind "which enlightens every man that cometh into the world," and his so-called individuality or personality consists of nothing but the manner in which he relates with the whole.

The law of attraction is impersonal and operates for all in a very effective manner. It is clear, therefore, that thoughts of abundance will respond only to similar thoughts; the wealth of the individual is seen to be what he or she inherently is. Affluence within is found to be the secret of attraction for affluence without. The ability to produce is found to be the real source of wealth of the individual. It is for this reason that the person who has their heart in their work and entertaining RIGHT LIVELIHOOD "as the Buddhists say" is certain to meet with unbounded success. The person will give and continually give; and the more that's given, the more received.

In this Module, please concentrate upon your power to create; seek insight, perception; try to find a logical basis for the faith which is in you. Let the thought dwell on the fact that the physical being lives and moves and has being in the sustainer of all organic life air, that the being must breathe to live.

Then, let the thought rest on the fact that the spiritual person also lives and moves and has being in a similar but subtler energy upon which the being must depend for life. And that, as in the physical world, no life assumes form <u>until after a seed is sown</u>, and no higher fruit except that of the parent stock can be produced. So in the spiritual world, no effect can be produced until the seed is sown and the fruit will depend upon the nature of the seed, so that the results which you secure depend upon your perception of law in the mighty domain of causation, the highest evolution of human consciousness. Since you are part of ALL, you rightfully may coexist harmoniously with ALL to increase your power, energy and spirit.

MODULE NINETEEN

The way to overcome fear is to become conscious of power, truth, prosperity, abundance and peace. What is this mysterious vital force which we call power? We do not know, but then, neither do we know what electricity is. And, we do know that by conforming to the requirements of the law by which electricity is governed, it will be our obedient servant; that it will light our homes, our cities, run our machinery, and serve us in many useful capacities.

And so it is - with vital force. Although we do not know what it is, and possibly may never know, we do know that it is a primary force which manifests through living bodies, and that by complying with the laws and principles by which it is governed, we can open ourselves to a more abundant inflow of this vital energy, and thus express the highest possible degree of mental, moral, and spiritual efficiency.

This part tells of a very simple way of developing this vital force. If you put into practice the information outlined in this lesson you will soon develop the sense of power which has been the distinguishing mark of the genius.

For your exercise this module, concentrate, and when I use the word concentrate, I mean all that the word implies; become so absorbed in the goal or object of your desires and thought that you are conscious of nothing else, and do this a few minutes every day. You take the necessary time to eat in order that the body may be nourished, why not take the time to assimilate your mental food? Take a few deep breaths. Think of optimal thoughts. Let the thought rest on the fact that appearances are deceptive. See beyond what is apparent. Attempt to see the good in everything. The earth is not flat, neither is it stationary; the sky is not a dome, the sun does not move, the stars are not small specks of light, and matter which was once supposed to be fixed has been found to be in a state of perpetual flux.

MODULE TWENTY

For many years there has been an endless discussion as to the origin of failure and negative circumstances. Theologians have told us that God is Love, and that God is Omnipresent. If this is true, there is no place where God is not.

> *God is Spirit. Spirit is the Creative Principle of the Universe. Man is made in the image and likeness of God. Man is therefore a spiritual being. The only activity which spirit possesses is the power to think. Thinking is therefore a creative process. All form is therefore the result of the thinking process. The destruction of form must also be a result of the thinking process. Invention, organization and constructive work of all kinds are the result of the creative power of thought, as in concentration. When the creative power of thought is manifested for the benefit of humanity, we call the result good. When the creative power of thought is manifested in a destructive manner, we call the result bad.*

This indicates the origin of both good and bad; they are simply words which have been coined in order to indicate the nature of the result of the thinking or creative process.

Thought necessarily precedes and predetermines action; action precedes and predetermines condition.

For your exercise this module, go into the Silence and concentrate on the fact that "In him, we live and move and have our being" is literally and scientifically exact! That you ARE because He IS, that if He is Omnipresent He must be in you. That if He is all in all - you must be in Him! That He is Spirit and you are made in "His image and likeness" and that the only difference between His spirit and your spirit is one of degree, that a part must be the same in kind and quality as the whole. When you can realize this clearly you will have found the secret of the creative power of thought, you will have found the origin of both good and bad, you will have found the secret of the wonderful power of concentration, you will have found the key to the solution of every problem whether physical, financial, or environmental.

MODULE TWENTY-ONE

You will find that everything which we hold in our consciousness for any length of time becomes impressed upon our subconsciousness and so becomes a pattern which the creative energy will wave into our life and environment. This is the secret of the wonderful power of prayer.

We know that the universe is governed by law; that for every effect there must be a cause, and that the same cause, under the same conditions, will invariably produce the same effect. Consequently, if prayer has ever been answered, it will always be answered, if the proper conditions are complied with. This must necessarily be true; otherwise the universe would be a chaos instead of a cosmos. The answer to prayer is therefore subject to law, and this law is definite, exact and scientific, just as are the laws governing gravitation and electricity. An understanding of this law takes the foundation of Christianity out of the realm of superstition and credulity and places it upon the firm rock of scientific understanding.

But, unfortunately, there are comparatively few persons who know how to pray. <u>They understand that there are laws governing electricity, mathematics, and chemistry, but, for some inexplicable reason, it never seems to occur to them that there are also spiritual laws, and that these laws are also definite, scientific, exact, and operate with immutable precision.</u>

This mental attitude is our personality and is composed of the thoughts which we have been creating in our own mind; therefore, if we wish a change in conditions all that is necessary is to change our thought; this will in turn change our mental attitude, which will in turn change our personality, which will in turn change the people, things and conditions, or, the experiences with which we meet in life.

For your exercise this Module, concentrate on the Truth Of Universal Laws. Try to realize that the Truth shall make you free, that is, nothing can permanently stand in the way of your perfect success when you learn to apply the scientifically correct thought methods and principles. Realize that you are externalizing in your environment your inherent soul potencies. Realize that the Silence offers an ever available and almost unlimited opportunity for awakening the highest conception of Truth. Try to comprehend that Omnipotence itself is absolute silence, all else is change, activity, limitation. Silent thought concentration is therefore the true method of reaching, awakening, and then expressing the wonderful potential power of the world within.

MODULE TWENTY-TWO

In Part Twenty-two, you will find that thoughts are spiritual seeds, which, when planted in the subconscious mind, have a tendency to sprout and grow, but unfortunately the fruit is frequently not to our liking.

Generally, the various forms of inflammation, paralysis, nervousness and diseased conditions are the manifestation of fear, worry, care, anxiety, jealousy, hatred and similar thought. The life processes are carried on by two distinct methods; first, the taking up and making use of nutritive material necessary for constructing cells; second, breaking down and excreting the waste material.

All life is based upon these constructive and destructive activities, and as food, water and air are the only requisites necessary for the construction of cells, it would seem that the problem of prolonging life indefinitely would not be a very difficult one.

However strange it may seem, it is the second or destructive activity that is, with rare exception, the cause of all disease. The waste material accumulates and saturates the tissues, which causes autointoxication. This may be partial or general. In the first case the disturbance will be local; in the second place it will affect the whole system.

The problem, then, before us in the healing of disease is to increase the inflow and distribution of vital energy throughout the system, and this can only be done by eliminating thoughts of fear, worry, care, anxiety, jealousy, hatred, and every other destructive thought, which tend to tear down and destroy the nerves and glands which control the excretion and elimination of poisonous and waste matter.

Many of you are very well balanced on a spiritual level. If you find that your life has been one of failure or that you are at a standstill, you may consider working with an analyst, therapist, life coach or counselor. This work you do with them would be to determine your faults, mistakes, fears, jealousies and resentments. You should verbally work through your personal history and misdeeds to clear out the past, dissipate guilt, comprehend your remorse, diffuse your frustration, and make room for constructive thinking.

This process has been referred to as a mental inventory in which you discard the destructive thinking such as resentments and open the door for abundance and prosperity. In general, it is YOUR job to engage character building. Overall, this process will free your mind and allow it to focus and work for you in conjunction with the Universe. In sum, it is difficult to be in a state of gratitude, thankfulness, faith or confident expectation when you harbor a bitter heart or an angry mind.

MODULE TWENTY-THREE

In this section, you will find that money weaves itself into the entire fabric of our very existence; that the law of success is service; that we get what we give, and for this reason we should consider it a great privilege to be able to give. Service includes giving of your time, your insight, your money, your energy and your love and support. Further, service would encompass people who create things that help society and the world...

We have found that thought is the creative activity behind every constructive enterprise. We can therefore give nothing of more practical value than our thought. Creative thought requires attention, and the power of attention is, as we have found, the weapon of the Super-human. Attention may be given to the supreme, to thankfulness, to you desires, to your relationships, to your career, to your health and so on. Attention develops concentration, and concentration develops Spiritual Power, and Spiritual Power is the mightiest force in existence.

This is the science that embraces all sciences. It is the art which, above all arts, is relevant to human life. In the mastery of this science and this art there is opportunity for unending progression. Perfection in this is not acquired in six days, nor in six weeks, nor in six months. It is the labor of life. Not to go forward is to go backward. Growth as a spiritually whole person is imperative.

It is inevitable that the entertainment of positive, constructive and unselfish thoughts should have a far-reaching effect for good. Compensation is the key-note of the universe. Nature is constantly seeking to strike equilibrium. Where something is sent out something must be received; else there should be a vacuum formed. By observance of this rule you cannot fail to profit in such measure as to amply justify your effort along this line. As man must be considered as a manifestation of Spirit; there is nothing sacrilegious in the idea that we, being Spirit, should so harmonize ourselves with his Origin and Source that he would be able to manifest at least a minor degree of its Power.

After this module, concentrate on the fact that a human being is not a body with a spirit, but a spirit with a body, and that it is for this reason that desires are incapable of any permanent satisfaction in anything not spiritual. Money is therefore of no value except to bring about the conditions which we desire, and these conditions are necessarily harmonious. Harmonious conditions necessitate sufficient supply, so that if there appears to be any lack, we should realize that the idea or soul of money is service, and as this thought takes form, channels of supply will be opened, and you will have the satisfaction of knowing that spiritual methods are entirely practical.

MODULE TWENTY-FOUR

If you have practiced each of the exercises a few minutes every day, as suggested, you will have found that you can get out of life exactly what you wish by first putting into life that which you wish, and you will probably agree with the student who said: "The thought is almost overwhelming, so vast, so available, so definite, so reasonable and so usable."

The fruit of this knowledge is, as it were, a gift of the Gods; it is the "truth" that makes men free, not only free from every lack and limitation, but free from sorrow, worry and care, and, is it not wonderful to realize that this law discriminates against no person, that it makes no difference what your habit of thought may be, the way has been prepared.

If you are inclined to be religious, the greatest religious teacher the world has ever known made the way so plain that all may follow. If your mental bias is toward physical science, the law will operate with mathematical certainty. If you are inclined to be philosophical, Plato or Emerson may be your teacher, but in either case, you may reach degrees of power to which it is impossible to assign any limit.

An understanding of this principle, I believe, is the secret for which the ancient Alchemists vainly sought, because it explains how gold in the mind may be transmuted into gold in the heart and in the hand.

After this module, try to realize that this is truly a wonderful world in which we live, that you are a wonderful being that many are awakening to a knowledge of the Truth, and as fast as they awake and come into a knowledge of the "things which have been prepared for them" they, too, realize that "Eye hath not seen, nor ear heard, neither hath it entered into the heart of man," the splendors which exist for those who find themselves in the Promised Land. They have crossed the river of judgment and have arrived at the point of discrimination between the true and the false, and have found that all they ever willed or dreamed, was but a faint concept of the dazzling reality.

"Though an inheritance of acres may be bequeathed,
an inheritance of knowledge and wisdom cannot.
The wealthy man may pay others for doing his work for him,
but it is impossible to get his thinking done for him
by another or to purchase any kind of self-culture."
- S. Smiles (Self Help - 1882)

Each student should focus on these steps:

1. What are your desires? Define them.
2. Are you willing to write our what you want to be and what you want for yourself. Can you be specific. Can you ask for more that you ever believed you could achieve?
3. Can you envision achieving them? Try and see them vividly.
4. Do you have the ability to select a definite goal and purpose to complete? Can you specify what you desire in concrete forms on paper and in the spoken word?
5. Are you willing to engage a harmonious relationship with the world and universe? Can you be thankful on a daily basis?
6. Are you willing to take action? Can you begin your dream? Are you willing to ask others for insight, cooperation and help?
7. Are you willing to focus and concentrate on constructive ideals and goals? Can you give your attention to one primary aspiration all day every day? Can you give your all – day in and day out to your ideal or goal?
8. Can you affirm to yourself verbally and with mental images the successful completion of your desires?
9. Are you willing to consider yourself worthy of having a full and rich life. Can you arrange your affairs so that you can receive what you earn or gifts of grace and prosperity.
10.   Is it possible for you to believe that you have possession of your desires NOW and IN THIS MOMENT as if you actually HAVE them…. Can you imagine yourself owning, being, or having what you really want. Why not?
11.   Can you live, speak and act in a constructive way in which your words, thoughts and actions are in concordance with prosperity, abundance, and peace.
12.   Are you willing to be grateful for the things you have and the things you do not have yet?
13.   Are you willing to engage your desires and passions with emotions of love and gratitude.
14.   Can you practice seeing what you want in your minds eye on a regular basis.

MODULE TWENTY-FIVE THROUGH TWENTY EIGHT –
OBSERVATIONS

The wisdom in the first 24 MODULES must be analyzed in the totality of life's circumstances. Each person is unique with varying talents and abilities, and ALL people have talent and abilities to be cultivated and honed on the mental, spiritual, and physical planes. All persons have a divine right to live, prosper and love in an abundant and creative environment. All things are possible with desire, faith, love, harmonious action and constructive thinking. It should be remembered that these steps below are important in our quest for excellence and peace. Take the best ideas from the list below and use them to improve your life:

1. The use of concentration and focus in your endeavors is vital. "Right Now" is the only moment in time that you HAVE to LIVE and to be of service. Not yesterday and not tomorrow.
2. Waste must be eliminated or transformed. Non-useful mental energies, thoughts and actions should be processed, avoided, or eliminated. Further, the body is Your temple; thus, you should consider the most constructive engagement of activities to revitalize and improve your body, mind and soul.
3. Cycles of growth and life occur. You may go through phases of struggle, challenge, strengthening, and transcendence. Analyze the cycles of your life.   Your growth leads to greater abilities, lessons learned, & knowledge.
4. Your body desires "life force". One of the ways to achieve greater life force is through breathing, meditation, and exercise. There are multitudes of activities and exercise that induce breathing, rejuvenation and the building of mental, spiritual, and physical fitness. It is your job to contemplate how to best accomplish this.
5. Staying connected with the source and forces of the Universe requires willingness. This connection also affords you stronger abilities to propel mind thought into the universe through prayer, contemplation, meditation or concentration.

6. The character of your thought is YOU. What you think is your reality. Your perception and peace of mind is governed by the quality and harmonious nature of your thought.
7. Love and spiritual harmony is the missing ingredient to success. Your thoughts attract like thoughts. Your thoughts and desires mixed with feeling-emotion and blended with love will manifest opportunities and blessings. You will serve humanity and achieve your highest good with the use of Love Energy and Love Thought. Sometimes love energy can be equated with your sexual magnetism also. The good news is that sexual magnetism and love energy can be harnessed and directed into your relationships, success, growth and other areas in a constructive way.
8. You determine your conscious relation to "ALL that IS" including people, places, things & the universal spirit. Your conscious thoughts are vibrations that surround you and vibrations sent out into the world. Harmonious thoughts will attract people toward you.
9. Blessings, focus, praise and gratitude directed toward anything or anyone will tend to bring that person or thing into your life. Thus, what you focus on expands. What is not important to you will tend to leave you, and this includes people, things, spirit force, or different types of thinking.
10. Surround yourself with experts and those who understand your desires. Form win-win relationships. As you give, you will receive in return.
11. Be aware of opportunities. People will offer proposals and ideas. You must be ready and willing to receive or use them.
12. Communication is key. Learn to speak, write, and communicate with others about your goals. Learn to ask for help, follow through, and give and receive to facilitate a more abundant life.
13. Learn to love yourself as worthy of all the good that the universe has to offer. Speak, act and do "AS IF" you are worthy. Do NOT discuss your past difficulties, faults or other negative circumstances. If you must, do it with a spiritual advisor or analyst.

14.   For specific goals and desires, try to relax and imagine the specific desire as you want it, as if you have it, detailing the picture on your mental screen, capturing the emotion, and harvesting the essence of the desire. Feel the joy of fulfilling the desire and love the thought of it unfolding. Hold the thought images clearly and often to further develop your thoughts.

15.   Remember that truth can be more than meets the eye. Try and see beyond what is apparent. Sometimes the eventual outcomes of your plans are better that you could have imagined.

16.   Action is the catalyst to propel your mental and spiritual advances. As you enhance and advance at all spiritual levels, your intuition and mind thoughts will guide you to do more and more toward the fulfillment of your desires. You will achieve things one by one effectively which leads you to your highest good.

17.   Waking up from the 3rd dimensional dream-state world and recognizing you are finally in the 4th dimension of co-creation with the universe is the fruit of our research, reading, and exercise of these principles. You are now master of your destiny in harmony and cooperation with the source of ALL and the universe.

18.   Flowing from all of these steps and suggestions, these blessings will allow you to guide and help others. You give of yourself & teach others so that you can keep your flow with the universe and fullness of life.

MODULE TWENTY-NINE - BONUS SECTION ON THE SCIENCE OF GETTING RICH AND WATTLES:

It is arguable that the definition of wealth is the free and unrestricted use of all of the things which may be necessary for you to advance in the direction of your dreams and potential thus attaining your fullest mental, spiritual, and physical prosperity.

You have a right to wealth because it is simply a desire for you to have a richer, fuller and more abundant life. We all should live for the equal advancement and fulfillment of body, mind and soul and there is no reason we should limit our capacities in any of the three sectors. Many people see greed, lust, and arrogance in the rich, and wonder if any wealthy people are truly happy. Ironically, poverty can and will frustrate your relationships with the spirit, people and those you love. Further, poverty creates a negative self-esteem, confidence and outlook upon life. With poverty of mind and life, you may have nothing to give to those you love and care about which leads to a very limited life and ability to connect to people and the world. Remember, giving is a form of love and compassion. In sum, abundance and wealth are the same, and if we recognize it and get in tune with it, prosperity will show itself in each of our lives.

If you are complacent with your life, then this philosophy is not for you. Stay where you are. Do not advance. Do not exercise your talents to the fullest. Do not leave your gift, mark or legacy to the world in the form of improvements, opportunity or education for all. However, if you want more out of life, and you are tired of failure, we will give you the secrets to success and the keys to prosperity. Why would or should you sit idly by and reject of deny the abundance of the world when it awaits your cooperation and seeking.

The world is plentiful with resources and your creativity is one of the many secrets to your future success. You do not need money to start something, to plan, to begin. You do not need a special talent or to save every penny to be rich. You do not need the perfect business location for your offices. Many people become rich with no talent, no college education, a less than perfect place to work and live, and no start-up capital.

The time is now to change your mind about life and to begin anew. When you are ready and willing to change and open your heart and mind, the goldmine of abundance will be available to you. The whole world of past and present has its eyes on you waiting for you to achieve your dreams, and all you need to do is make the mental and spiritual shift in consciousness.

There is plenty of opportunity. Creativity, innovation, and abundance will go to the people who flow and cooperate with life and not reject it. Nature has an inexhaustible source of riches. Accordingly, it is natural to seek more from life, and your advancement is vital for growth. As the old adage states, "We grow or die". On the higher plane and dimension, a person can make 40 years worth of advances in 3-6 years with efficient work. For example, the last 100 years has shown more life and technological improvements that the last 2000 years of civilization.

We will now show you the first secret of life. This key to success can be yours if you simply accept the following statement. Just take it as fact, and the world will begin to move with you.

THOUGHT PRECEEDS FORM

You conceive of your desire, you believe that your goal will happen, and you retrieve the opportunity from the world's storehouse of riches. As a rule, man originates thought. Thought turns into plans or mental images in the mind. Man can communicate his thought and mental images into and throughout the world. This creation begins with our thought focused within and without.

Your mind is the center of your world. The presence of the universal spirit can be allowed into your mind. Your thoughts mixed with a thankful heart directed toward your inner presence can flow out into the world. You picture and believe that your healthy goal is possible. You understand the essence and reasons that you should have this type of result in your life. You picture your goal with specificity. You think of and picture the opportunity frequently. You believe that you have the type of result that you desire. You feel it and harvest the emotion of having it as much as possible. These thoughts and a mental practice of visualization will send off into the world like a letter of request. If you practice this visualization enough, the desires you have will be met. Truth is your faithful non-doubting interpretation of your thoughts. Do not focus on failure, poverty, disease, or lack. Your truth is health, riches, success, and happiness. Do not doubt your thoughts and dreams. Do not speak against them. Keep these mental petitions as faithful as possible while living harmonious with people, places, institutions and the universe.

It is the desire of the universal spirit that you should have all that your need. You will begin with a simple desire for some type of improvement in life. A desire coupled with unwavering faith will correctly unfold for you over time. The motives of your desires are important: You want to help yourself and others, and you do not want to hurt other people.
You will achieve these desires much quicker if your motives are not colored in greed, ego, pride, lust, competition, hate, resentment, and arrogance. Your desires must be propelled by love, gratitude, faith, confidence, mental focus, truth, acceptance, creativity, positive expectation, clear planning, & giving more love and value than you take.

TO BEGIN YOUR PROCESS OF PROSPERITY

Brainstorm on your ideas each day. Clarify in you mind exactly what you want and how you will achieve it. Hold the picture of the moment you have completed the achievement with positive certainty. Never speak or think of it as not being possible. Claim it as yours, claim the picture of success as a "FACT" and that it is already yours in mind. Keep your mind tuned in to the universal presence and energy by having a thankful heart and grateful thoughts. If you can not be grateful; then, begin to think of your ability to walk, talk, see, hear, travel, speak, etc. The simplest of freedoms to be grateful for are the most easily overlooked. But, these abilities such as your health are the quickest way to show gratitude and begin a new and powerful positive outlook that connects you to life and your dreams. People will soon not recognize your new outlook and serenity. Remember, that you must exercise this mental picturing and thankfulness every day for at least a month. However, after a month, you will not believe the difference in your perception of life.

Do not be scared or ashamed to ask for what you really want. Ask for more than you need. The world is full of people to give and receive. Never be scared to receive. Receive with humility, thankfulness and appreciation. Extreme poverty and self-sacrifice are not pleasing to anyone, and extreme altruism is just is dangerous and extreme greed or piety. Thus, give and receive with joy.

We believe that there is a universal spirit of which unlimited abundance flows. It will give us all that we need and desire when we have a pure heart. A pure heart and mind simply means that you do not allow the weeds of ignorance, bitterness, hate, and irritation cloud and fill your mind. To facilitate a mind of purity, we make the profound connection to the universal spirit within us by developing a strong feeling of thankfulness for life, love, health, and our material gifts that we already have or will have.

Let us think about gratitude and thankfulness. Can you have happiness with a bitter heart? Can you have real faith when you are constantly blaming, angry and ungrateful? If you think you can be happy with a blaming, hateful, and bitter mind, then, good luck. If you want to change to an outlook on life where you feel that all is possible, then keep reading.

Think back and reflect on the times in your life where you got what you wanted and became arrogant or ego centered. After you got what you wanted or got out of a jam, you forgot about and abandoned your connection to your universal spirit. You may have given up your connection o the spirit and world because you thought you had won the game of life. When good things happen to you is the EXACT time that you should exercise and practice having grateful thoughts to continue the flow of riches to us. What you focus on expands. What becomes important to you will come to you and remain with you. If you have doubt and fear, your gratitude will dispel fear and doubt. Gratitude will keep you connected to the world and affords you a harmonious relationship with all. Gratitude and thankfulness prevents dissatisfaction. Continue to fix your attention on thanks and the best in life. Fix you mind on health, love, success, and good fortune. Your faith will be renewed and strengthened from your exercise of gratitude. It may not happen over night, but within a month of this simple 5 minute a day practice, you WILL have results. As an exercise, go a week without complaining. As you may know, complaining attracts destructive people, places and things into your life. Each time you find yourself complaining, touch each of your shoulders with your finger, and proclaim, "I am abundance".

If you have trouble with certain negative triggers, then eliminate them. If government bothers you, then quit reading the paper for a while. If certain people constantly annoy you, then you should avoid them for a time too. You are working on yourself, and it is OK to take care of your well-being first. The people around you will be happy in the end, if you rebuild and renew your positive spirit and enthusiasm for life as a priority. This is putting your health first i.e. your spiritual health.

Your desires should be very specific. Your mental blueprint must be just as precise. For example, as an exercise, you may write out on a piece of paper a personal contract to yourself:

I <u>John Doe, Jr.</u> will have a million dollar business 4 years from today. I will sell creative WIDGETS. I will give the best service and value to my clients. My products and services have outstanding benefits and will help all of my customers. I will do all of these things, work hard, and be persistent in my service and quality. I will not give up. People will be glad to pay me for my services because they are a benefit to the customer. I will gladly accept payment and do what I need to do to receive the compensation.
OR

I, John Doe, Jr. desire a better job position in the field of (xxxxxxx). I will work hard and do a great job in my present position. In the meantime, evenings, or weekends, I will learn more about the type of job that I desire and improved opportunities. Further, I will hone my skills, interviewing abilities, and improve myself. I see myself in a great job and in a harmonious position. I will also communicate with potential employers, research positions and make applications for those jobs. In 3 months, I will have a better position with better pay with another company or my present company.

Spend each day contemplating your personal agreement. Visualize the million-dollar business or the better job. Form a specific and clear mental image of the new job and position or of you being paid ONE MILLION DOLLARS FOR THE BUSINESS in the form of a check or stock. Mentally imagine yourself on that very moment of completing the transaction with joy. Feel it, harvest the emotion, and believe that an outcome or even better outcome is possible.

The clearer the picture, the stronger the desire. If your desire is strong, your willingness to focus on the success and claiming it as yours will be made a seamless transaction. You must engage your heart felt faith to secure a small step to success in each day. Stay busy and keep moving toward your goals with gratitude and faith. After you have pictured your optimal vision and read your personal agreement to yourself, complete the meditative thought process with the words "AND IT IS SO, THANK YOU FOR THE BLESSING, THANK YOU FOR EXPANDING THE QUALITY OF MY LIFE, AND THANK YOU FOR PROTECTING ME AND MY FAMILY" This will complete your exercise and you then send this petition into the world like a request that must be granted, and you should be ready to receive it.

You need only use your willingness on yourself. You need not think of adversely harming others. You may then always use your self-will to force yourself to think about certain constructive things and doing certain beneficial actions. Every moment in doubt is a waste of time. Direct your attention to prosperity. The best thing you can do for the non-believers is to show them that you can achieve abundance and success. Your creative idea and plan WILL be a success if it is a strong desire that you are willing to go the distance to fulfill.

Do not tell the same old doubtful people of your plans and ideas. If you tell enough bitter people about your idea, their collective doubt may doom and sabotage your dreams. Surround yourself with experts in the field, people who are encouraging and insightful, people working toward a new outlook on life. Do not sink into the past by telling others about your difficulties or failures (unless in a secure peer-group where you have at least an unwritten contract of privacy and support). Interest yourself in becoming rich in life! Always try to see the positive side of your present state of affairs. Focus on optimistic conversation or beneficial events that have happened in your life.

When you are willing, you must act the part. Do what you need to do. Make lists of things to do and begin doing them one by one. It may take a year to complete, but we must begin somewhere. Do each series of tasks and individual actions efficiently. Do them right the first time, and you need not fix it later. To do efficient and effective work, you only need to do one thing at a time and do not spread yourself too thin. You need not try and mandate an outcome. The creative forces will unfold the correct and highest result for you. You merely need to organize your affairs so that you may receive the success and gladly accept the payoff. Overall, action is what will allow you to receive your abundance. Do only what can be done today, and tomorrow you can begin anew. In sum, put the faith, vision, and purpose behind your every action to accelerate your reaching higher abundance.

FIND OUT WHAT YOU REALLY WANT TO DO AND BE!

You should determine what you like or even what you love to do through this simple process. Write out a list of 20 things of interest to you. Continue adding and subtracting from the list. Over time, you will only have 2 or 3 things left because the supreme power will guide you toward your highest given talents. As a note, your purpose could be to study history or science, to read books, to write, to develop written content, to draw or create art and graphics, to travel, to communicate with people. It should over time become more specific such as: I intend to become the best speaker or writer on the topic of politics or taxes, to complete a masters or doctorate in international business, to build the best website for information and links to success literature. It does not matter how you start, just begin the writing process!

Just remember, a good talent (something you like to do and you are good at doing) combined with desire to become the best professional in this field will guarantee that you do and be what you love. At the least, you can become a teacher of your trade or profession and give back to the world by accelerating the learning of children or students in your field of love.

Without being boastful, you must convey the impression to others that you are advancing all that come in contact with you. Covey to others that you can add to their lives to promote your goals and ideals. Speak of your life and business as getting better and better all of the time. Act and feel as though you are very successful and that you are already rich in life and all of your needs are met. Incorporate a compassionate humility that you mix with poise, faith, confidence, and self-esteem. You need only speak when necessary, but your strong character and faithful confidence will attract the best people into your life.

If you are in a job and you cannot leave it to immediately follow your dreams, then do what you can in the evenings or weekends to hone your skills, plans, and education toward your goal. Use your present job skillfully to move in the direction that you want. There are thousands of people who have their business pay for their part-time education. Your contacts at work may lead to a better or different job. You must be prepared to discuss your dreams (what you want from life) in spoken words. You must know exactly what you want, and you must clarify and quantify it to others. You must be able to ask for and accept what you want out of life. You will need to interact with others who can help you. This process of abundance, harmonization and advancement will lead others to want to help you. Be ready for them and be open to forming alliances with them. Thus, your visions, meditations, and requests are traditionally answered by the universal power in the form of another person or entity being available to help and guide you. Be READY to tell them what you need, and do not be ashamed to ask for a win-win relationship with the people that come to you.

In conclusion, times are only as good as your mind perceives them. Just when you think you are failing is the exact time to continue your gratitude, meditation on you goals, and ACTION! Just at that moment of doubt is when the highest good for you is ready to unfold. Even if the result isn't exactly as you want, something better is very close and coming to you, and you have only been protected from a bad deal or relationship by waiting a little longer

METAPHYSICAL ISSUES & INSIGHTS

Harmonious Relationships:

Connected with all there is that is good, harvesting and having a harmonious relationship with the world through various philosophical exercises, using gratitude for any of your gifts on a daily basis can grow your expectation of good and faith. It is much easier to be connected when you have set aside or removed destructive thinking such as resentments, jealously or the seven deadly sins.

Desires

Desires are good and excellent. Desires can focus you on enriching your life and following your true direction. Cultivating desires into reality is vital for change, innovation, and improvement. You would not have a desire unless it was possible, but select desires where you have a solid sphere of possibility. An earnest and heartfelt desire is what allows us to seize upon opportunities and develop plans.

Plans

A plan or objective is fundamental in the clarification and specificity of your desire. A large majority of people are afraid to specify what they intend to do. Transcending this fear and taking bold action upon your plans and strategies allows for the growth and manifestation of your idea into a reality.

Vision

A vision is important in that you clarify the path to your short-term and long-term enrichment of yourself, your goals, teamwork, or relationships.

Mission

A mission is important in that you can quantify and clarify a path to an outcome or ending strategy.

Having, Emotion, and Feelings

Mentally understanding the outcome or result as if you have it already is very important. It also allows you to qualify the consequences. It further provides you with feelings surrounding the outcome. Harvesting positive feelings surrounding the outcome is very important to energize a desire, mission, visualization, and result.

Visualization, Pictures, Imagination, Sending It Out

Mental visualization of your objectives holds great importance in the clarity of what you intend to do along the way and what you desire as an end result. Seeing what you intend to do and what you desire and plan as if it is real is a complex mental exercise, but vital to the codification and building of the objective so as to assist the manifestation of the result. Seeing *exactly* what you desire and intend causes you to specify your wants and desires. The stronger and longer you can hold your ideal in your mind's eye, the better.

Attention Focus

Pointing your mental faculties toward the individual actions required to achieve a task, project, or goal is what causes effectiveness, as long as your acts are efficient. Continuous and persistent thinking and action toward your work, goal, project, or desired outcome can funnel or intensify the energy in a specific direction.

Efficiently and Effectively

Completion and closure of acts and tasks one-by-one in a successful manner is what creates momentum toward an objective with no need to go backward.

Presence, Awareness, Doing

Thinking and planning are most crucial. However, boldness and action are what may cause events to happen and people to be attracted to you. Therefore, contemplation mixed with action is the optimal, blended solution.

Cause/Effect: "Like Attracts Like"

Every action has a reaction. Types of actions and thoughts attract similar actions and thoughts. Kindness tends to bring kindness. Respect tends to bring respect. Additionally, constructive thinking tends to bring constructive opportunities and events to the individual.

Increase

All mankind tends to be attracted to those who can bring them more life or enrichment. If an individual projects life and opportunity, then he or she will attract similar minds.

Insight and Restraint

Insight and restraint contain the ability to think something over, discuss it with others, or seek out counsel from others who understand or know the subject well without acting hastily. Thus, the opinion of experts and consequences are a valid consideration in thinking and acting.

Love, Forgiveness, Harmony, Dissipating Discouragement

Cultivating love and forgiveness can dispel otherwise destructive thoughts. Great minds can look back on things they love or loved, and re-harness that emotion.

Minding Your Own Business

There is something very real in taking care of yourself and your affairs. As such, your enhanced mind, body, soul, and financial affairs allow you to help those whom you love and serve humanity in better ways. The best way to be of service to humanity and your loved ones is to make the best of yourself.

Gratitude, Enthusiasm, Faith

A sincere heartfelt gratitude for life and its gifts will allow the flow of good to you. Systematic recognition of people or things to be thankful for along with gratitude may facilitate an expectation of good and growth of inherent faith. Integrating this confident expectation with your aspirations creates great power.

Guarded Speech, Response/Ability

Speaking of only positive things can attract opportunity and friends. Keeping your desires and goals close to you will keep them from becoming dissipated energy. Sharing your desires and goals with those who support, encourage, and assist you can be a positive exercise and help harvest constructive feedback.

Change/Insanity

Not evolving while continuing to do things that are failures or destructive actions tends to prevent any growth.

Creating Versus Competing

It seems that many people feel that competition causes a limited supply. However, from a supply or abundance standpoint, individuals can create without competing, to serve humanity. As an example, an individual who creates a new cure to solve a common health problem is not competing against the world, but helping it.

Right Livelihood and Labor of Love

Having a labor of love can cause effectiveness and efficiency through energetic work. Doing something that you believe in or selling a product that you have faith in, can make your job much easier or even fun. Having fun with work is a divine right.

Blessing, Praise, Protection, and Expansion

Persons who engage in a metaphysical approach seem to enjoy a greater state of well-being and success when they bless their relationship with the Universe, bless their loved ones, bless their home, and give thanks for their health on a daily basis.

Gratitude, Religion and Great Thinkers

If the only prayer you say in your life is "Thank you," that would suffice. --Meister Eckhart

Take full account of the excellencies which you possess, and in gratitude remember how you would hanker after them, if you had them not. --Marcus Aurelius

The Holy Koran, which is divided into sections called *suras*, repeatedly asserts the necessity for gratitude and thankfulness to God. For example, in Sura fourteen it is written: "If you are grateful, I will give you more "(14:7). A traditional Islamic saying states, "The first who will be summoned to paradise are those who have praised God in every circumstance." The prophet Muhammad also stated, "Gratitude for the abundance you have received is the best insurance that the abundance will continue." True gratitude, it is taught, draws more abundant graces upon the believer.

Judaism

In the Jewish faith, gratitude is a critical component of worship. In the Hebrew Scriptures, the Psalms are saturated with thanksgiving to God: "O Lord my God, I will give thanks to you forever" (30:12), and "I will give thanks to the Lord with my whole heart "(9:1).

Christianity

In the Christian faith, Philippians IV sums up the Christian attitude toward gratitude. See Below:

Philippians IV

4 Rejoice in the Lord always. Again I will say, rejoice! 5 Let your gentleness be known to all men. The Lord [is] at hand.   6 Be anxious for nothing, but in everything by prayer and supplication, with thanksgiving, let your requests be made known to God;   7 and the peace of God, which surpasses all understanding, will guard your hearts and minds through Christ Jesus.   8 Finally, brethren, whatever things are true, whatever things [are] noble, whatever things [are] just, whatever things [are] pure, whatever things [are] lovely, whatever things [are] of good report, if [there is] any virtue and if [there is] anything praiseworthy -- meditate on these things.   9 The things which you learned and received and heard and saw in me, these do, and the God of peace will be with you.

10 But I rejoiced in the Lord greatly that now at last your care for me has flourished again; though you surely did care, but you lacked opportunity.   11 Not that I speak in regard to need, for I have learned in whatever state I am, to be content: 12 I know how to be abased, and I know how to abound. Everywhere and in all things I have learned both to be full and to be hungry, both to abound and to suffer need.   13 I can do all things through Christ who strengthens me.

Read the above statements and passages from the Old Scriptures and other quotes and think about: gentleness, thanksgiving, constructive petitions, request for blessings, a sincere feeling of gratitude, meditating on noble and optimistic thoughts, rejoicing in life, and even blessing yourself and your future.

Unfolding Detachment Protected for Higher Good

When we become too attached or dependent on an external person, place, thing, or result, we can become disappointed with other people and things. It is good to expect the best, but it is also smart to allow for something better to unfold. Thus, trying to control a specific outcome without any flexibility can inhibit the Universe from its creativity.

Receiving, Valuing, Deserving

Many people from around the world feel unworthy of abundance. Many people do not value themselves, their service, their talents, and work. It is very important to learn to feel worthy, unique, and deserving of good. Moreover, you should become mentally open to receiving all good in life. Further, people should be careful to create ways to receive the good into their lives from the Universe and from others. Example: Accepting a compliment from another person.

Other People and When They Are Sent to Help You

When you engage a mentality of abundance and harmonious Spiritual thinking, your mind will expand and increase while radiating love, abundance, and health. Thus, your powers of attraction will increase. The Universe will send people to help you. It will be your job to select and allow them to assist you in a win-win relationship to expand your abundance where all can achieve a richer and fuller life through these joint ventures.

Resistance and Flow

Types of resistance that inhibit your abundance, health, and connection with Spirit are: resentment, jealousy, anger, judgment, criticism, hatred, greed, pride, and mental laziness. Other subtle resistance is to institutions, conformity, and adapting. It is better to adapt than to perish, while maintaining your unique qualities

Willingness

Willingness is the key to advancement. Be willing to take action, take a chance, or risk failure or embarrassment. Without willingness, you may never engage mental, Spiritual, or physical action that leads to good. Willingness is a vital ingredient toward successful visualization, belief, action, planning, and success. Am I willing to believe, to try, to risk, to engage? Can it be done? And why not?

Hoarding and Change

Holding onto old ideas, old things, and old ways can keep you from growth, Spiritual flow, and expansion. Taking an inventory of mental ideas and material things must be done. Eliminating the ideas, things, people, and actions that create inconvenience, frustration, clutter, and resentment will allow freedom and harmony in your life.

Recognition of Cause

It can be a fundamental mistake if you give yourself too much credit for anything good that you receive from life. Additionally, it can be a disastrous mistake to continue to blame God and the Universe for anything bad that you receive from life.

Sanity, Root Out Cause, Unlimited Potential

Root out the cause of your failures, your inconveniences, your frustration, and your mental or Spiritual disabilities. If you have a problem, there may be a cause. If you injured yourself engaging in a specific activity, you may avoid this activity in the future or better prepare for it next time. Otherwise, you may pay for this repeated action in the form of more pain and suffering. If you have a relationship that always seems to leave you in pain, then you may need to avoid this person if you are spiritually whole and the other person is not.

Giving Without Expectation, Tithing

Taking time to give money, service, or goods to divine recipients will create an untold flow in your life. Life requires circulation of your ideas, your things, and your service to humanity. With this giving, it is virtually guaranteed that your life will be blessed and protected through your giving of yourself. You are not doing this to take advantage of the law. You do this to expand your Spiritual existence, keep the flow, and give back. Expecting something in return is not needed because the Universe will provide opportunity for you by your embracing this process.

Wasting Energy and Thought

If you become frustrated every time you watch the news or read the newspaper, then why would you continue to read a specific article or watch that particular channel? It is vitally important for you to engage relaxing or strengthening activities rather than getting the same shot of bad medicine each day.

Good Deeds and Action / Balance Karma

You may feel you have wronged many people. You may even feel guilty for past deeds or encounters. However, if you feel remorse and intend to act as a better person for now on, then you have made progress. In any event, your day-to-day action and character of goodness and kindness will build your positive energy where the world has decided to protect you and serve you.

Meek Defined: Open Mind, Will of God, Spirit Before Ego

Meek is not weak. It is strong, confident, cooperative, and advantageous. Developing an honest appraisal of yourself can be healthy. You can always improve yourself, your credentials, your relationships and your business. Putting your ego first can be dangerous. When somebody has hurt your feelings, said you are wrong, said "no" to you, or otherwise attacked you, it is best to analyze (when possible) and discuss the issue with another supportive person before retaliating with e-mail, phone, letter, or in person.

Peace and Serenity Are Needed for Concentration

Peace allows growth. Clarity and concentration are primary keys to serenity. Being able to operate on a plane with singleness of mind can allow you to achieve great things. A person who cannot focus and achieve one thing at a time may never cross "the finish line" with any dream, goal, or aspiration. Overall, if you allow resentment, frustration, hate of another, or fear to dominate your thoughts, then your effectiveness will be diminished. Hard work is required to keep you focused and concentrating on bettering yourself. Overall, your freedom, vitality and wholeness depend on your effectiveness.

Visualizing Completed Transaction With Joy

We have mentioned visualization. Do not forget that you should visualize things and plans as you would have them. You should believe that they are yours in mind. Paint your ideal outcome on the mental screen in your mind's eye. Believe that it is completed. Fuse your image with love and gratitude. Celebrate its reception in your mind. Believe that you have the proper channels to receive what is coming to you. Send your vision and petition into the Universe and repeat the exercise for fantastic results.

Treasure Map and Wheel of Fortune

If you cannot paint the mental picture as clearly as you would want, then try to use the material world to enhance your mind. Cut out pictures of the ideal things you want. Put them into a collage or on poster board. Rip out images of the home you desire, people having fun, distant places that you want to visit, or the lifestyle and types of relationships that you desire. This action can help you amalgamate the images to imprint them on your subconscious mind. View them daily and place them in a prominent place. Overall, imagine having these things in your quite time. Sense the joy of receiving all of it fully.

Dr. CHARLES F. HAANEL, PhD, Psy. D. –THE MASTER KEY SYSTEM REVISITED & EXERCISES IN 24 PARTS – ABT. 1912

Introduction: Nature compels us all to move through life. We could not remain stationary however much we wished. Every right-thinking person wants not merely to move through life like a sound-producing, perambulating plant, but to develop - to improve - and to continue the development mentally to the close of physical life.

Some men seem to attract success, power, wealth, attainment, with very little conscious effort; others conquer with great difficulty; still others fail altogether to reach their ambitions, desires and ideals. Why is this so? Why should some men realize their ambitions easily, others with difficulty, and still others not at all?

1. The attitude of mind necessarily depends upon what we think. Therefore, the secret of all power, all achievement and all possession depends upon our method of thinking. The world without is a reflection of the world within. Harmony in the world within means the ability to control our thoughts, and to determine for ourselves how any experience is to affect us.

2. Our difficulties are largely due to confused ideas and ignorance of our true interests. Thought is energy. Active thought is active energy; concentrated thought is a concentrated energy. Thought concentrated on a definite purpose becomes power. This is the power which is being used by those who do not believe in the virtue of poverty, or the beauty of self-denial. They perceive that this is the talk of weaklings.The value of the subconscious is enormous; it inspires us; it warns us; it furnishes us with names, facts and scenes from the storehouse of memory. It directs our thoughts, tastes, and accomplishes tasks so intricate that no conscious mind, even if it had the power, has the capacity for. On the spiritual side, it is the source of ideals, of aspiration, of the imagination, and is the channel through which we recognize our Divine Source, and in proportion as we recognize this divinity do we come into an understanding of the source of power.

3. It is our attitude of mind toward life which determines the experiences with which we are to meet; if we expect nothing, we shall have nothing; if we demand much, we shall receive the greater portion. The world is harsh only as we fail to assert ourselves. The criticism of the world is bitter only to those who cannot compel room for their ideas. It is fear of this criticism that causes many ideas to fail to see the light of day.

Exercise: I want you to not only be perfectly still, and inhibit all thought as far as possible, but relax, let go, let the muscles take their normal condition; this will remove all pressure from the nerves, and eliminate that tension which so frequently produces physical exhaustion.

4. The greatest and most marvelous power which this "I" has been given is the power to think, but few people know how to think constructively, or correctly, consequently they achieve only indifferent results. Most people allow their thoughts to dwell on selfish purposes, the inevitable result of an infantile mind. When a mind becomes mature, it understands that the germ of defeat is in every selfish thought.

One of the strongest affirmations which you can use for the purpose of strengthening the will and realizing your power to accomplish, is, "I can be what I will to be." Every time you repeat it realize who and what this "I" is; try to come into a thorough understanding of the true nature of the "I"; if you do, you will become invincible; that is, provided that your objects and purposes are constructive and are therefore in harmony with the creative principle of the Universe.

5. In the domain of mind and spirit, in the domain of practical power, such an estate is yours. You are the heir! You can assert your heirship and possess, and use this rich inheritance. Power over circumstances is one of its fruits, and health, harmony and prosperity are assets upon its balance sheet. It offers you poise and peace. It costs you only the labor of studying and harvesting its great resources. It demands no sacrifice, except the loss of your limitations, your servitudes, your weakness. It clothes you with self-honor, and puts a scepter in your hands. To gain this estate, three processes are necessary: You must earnestly desire it. You must assert your claim. You must take possession.

Exercise: Now, go to your room, enter your relaxed state, and mentally select a place which has pleasant associations. Make a complete mental picture of it, see the buildings, the grounds, the trees, friends, associations, everything complete. At first, you will find yourself thinking of everything under the sun, except the ideal upon which you desire to concentrate. But do not let that discourage you. Persistence will win, but persistence requires that you practice these exercises every day without fail.

6. To be in tune with eternal truth we must possess poise and harmony within. In order to receive intelligence the receiver must be in tune with the transmitter. Every thought sets the brain cells in action; at first the substance upon which the thought is directed fails to respond, but if the thought is sufficiently refined and concentrated, the substance finally yields and expresses perfectly. Finding harmony with the universal power will bring you great power and resources.

7. Visualization is the process of making mental images, and the image is the mold or model which will serve as a pattern from which your future will emerge. Make the image clear and clean-cut, hold it firmly in the mind and you will gradually and constantly bring the thing nearer to you. You can be what "you will to be." You should see the end before a single step is taken; so you are to picture in your mind what you want; you are sowing the seed, but before sowing any seed you want to know what the harvest is to be.

This is Idealization. If you are not sure, return to the quiet meditation or prayer daily until the picture becomes plain. Make the Mental Image; make it clear, distinct, perfect; hold it firmly; the ways and means will develop; supply will follow the demand; you will be led to do the right thing at the right time and in the right way. Earnest Desire will bring about Confident Expectation, and this in turn must be reinforced by Firm Demand.

Exercise: Visualize a friend, see your friend exactly as you last saw him, see the room, the furniture, recall the conversation, now see his face, see it distinctly, now talk to him about some subject of mutual interest; see his expression change, watch him smile. Can you do this?

8. As the one purpose of life is growth, all principles underlying existence must contribute to give it effect. Thought, therefore, takes form and the law of growth eventually brings it into manifestation. You may freely choose what you think, but the result of your thought is governed by an immutable law. Any line of thought persisted in cannot fail to produce its result in the character, health and circumstances of the individual.

The law of attraction will certainly and unerringly bring to you the conditions, environment, and experiences in life, corresponding with your habitual, characteristic, predominant mental attitude. Not what you think once in a while when you are in church, or have just read in a good book, BUT your predominant mental attitude is what counts.

Combining harmonious thought and visualization with the great powers within is where true energy and creation comes from. Place yourself in position to receive this power. As it is Omnipresent, it must be within you. We know that this is so because we know that all power is from within, but it must be developed, unfolded, & cultivated; in order to do this we must be receptive and open.

9. Hold in mind the condition desired; affirm it as an already existing fact. This indicates the value of a powerful affirmation. By constant repetition it becomes a part of ourselves. We are actually changing ourselves; are making ourselves what we want to be.

To think correctly, accurately, we must know the "Truth." We must realize that truth is the vital principle of the Universal Mind and is Omnipresent. For instance, if you require health, a realization of the fact that the "I" in you is spiritual and that all spirit is one; that wherever a part is the whole must be, will bring about a condition of health, because every cell in the body must manifest the truth as you see it.

If you require Love try to realize that the only way to get love is by giving it, that the more you give the more you will get, and the only way in which you can give it, is to fill yourself with it, until you become a magnet.

If you require Wealth a realization of the fact that the "I" in you is one with the Universal mind which is all substance, and is Omnipotent, will assist you in bringing into operation the law of attraction which will bring you into vibration with those forces which make for success and bring about conditions of power and affluence in direct proportion with the character and purpose of your affirmation and thinking. The affirmation, "I am whole, perfect, strong, powerful, loving, harmonious and happy", will bring about harmonious conditions.

The reason for this is because the affirmation is in strict accordance with the Truth, and when truth appears every form of error or discord must necessarily disappear. You have found that the "I" is spiritual, it must necessarily then always be no less than perfect, the affirmation. "I am whole, perfect, strong, powerful, loving, harmonious and happy" is therefore an exact scientific statement.

Whatever you desire for yourself, affirm it for others, and it will help you both. We reap what we sow. If we send out thoughts of love and health, they return to us like bread cast upon the waters...

10. Abundance is a natural law of the Universe. The evidence of this law is conclusive; we see it on every hand. Everywhere Nature is lavish, wasteful, and extravagant.

The man who understands that there is no effect without an adequate cause thinks impersonally. He gets down to bedrock facts regardless of consequences.

Thought is the connecting link between the Infinite and the finite, between the Universal and the individual. Constructive thought must necessarily be creative, but creative thought must be harmonious, and this eliminates all destructive or competitive thought.

Exercise: Select a blank space on the wall, or any other convenient spot, from where you usually sit, mentally draw a black horizontal line about six inches long, try to see the line as plainly as though it were painted on the wall; now mentally draw two vertical lines connecting with this horizontal line at either end; now draw another horizontal line connecting with the two vertical lines; now you have a square. Try to see the square perfectly; when you can do so draw a circle within the square; now place a point in the center of the circle; now draw the point toward you about 10 inches; now you have a cone on a square base; you will remember that your work was all in black; change it to white, to red, to yellow.

Many fail because, they do not understand the law; there is no link to universal mind; they have not formed the connection. The remedy is a conscious recognition of the law of attraction with the intention of bringing the best into existence for a definite purpose. If done rightly, thought will correlate with its object (what you want) and bring it into manifestation, because thought is a product of the spiritual man, and spirit is the creative Principle of the Universe.

11. While every effect is the result of a cause, the effect in turn becomes a cause, which creates other effects, which in turn create still other causes; so that when you put the law of attraction into operation you must remember that you are starting a train of causation for good or otherwise which may have endless possibilities. We are first to believe that our desire has already been fulfilled, its accomplishment will then follow. This is a concise direction for making use of the creative power of thought by impressing on the Universal subjective mind, the particular thing which we desire as an already existing fact.

This conception is also elaborated upon by Swedenborg in his doctrine of correspondences; and a still greater teacher has said, "What things soever ye desire, when ye pray, believe that ye receive them, and ye shall have them." (Mark 11:24) The difference of the tenses in this passage is remarkable. "Faith is the substance of things hoped for, the evidence of things unseen." The Law of Attraction is the Law by which Faith is brought into manifestation. This law has eliminated the elements of uncertainty and caprice from men's lives and substituted law, reason, and certitude.

Exercise: Concentrate on the quotation taken from the Bible, "Whatsoever things ye desire, when ye pray, believe that ye receive them and ye shall have them"; notice that there is no limitation, "Whatsoever things" is very definite and implies that the only limitation which is placed upon us in our ability to think, to be equal to the occasion, to rise to the emergency, to remember that Faith is not a shadow, but a substance, "the substance of things hoped for, the evidence of things not seen."

12. "You must first have the knowledge of your power; second, the courage to dare; third, the faith to do." It is the combination of Thought and Love which forms the irresistible force, called the law of attraction. All natural laws are irresistible, the law of Gravitation, or Electricity, or any other law operates with mathematical exactitude.

The intention governs the attention. Things are created in the mental or spiritual world before they appear in the outward act or event by the simple process of governing our thought forces today, we help create the events which will come into our lives in the future, perhaps even tomorrow.

Exercise: Get into the same relaxed state in the same position as you were previously; let go, both mentally and physically; always do this; never try to do any mental work under pressure; see that there are no tense muscles or nerves, that you are entirely comfortable. Now realize your unity with omnipotence; get into touch with this power, come into a deep and vital understanding, appreciation, and realization of the fact that your ability to think is your ability to act upon the Universal Mind, and bring it into manifestation, realize that it will meet any and every requirement; that you have exactly the same potential ability which any individual ever did have or ever will have, because each is but an expression or manifestation of the One, all are parts of the whole, there is no difference in kind or quality, the only difference being one of degree.

13. Part Thirteen which follows tells why the dreams of the dreamer come true. It explains the law of causation by which dreamers, inventors, authors, financiers, bring about the realization of their desires. It explains the law by which the thing pictured upon our mind eventually becomes our own. Every individual who ever advanced a new idea, whether a Columbus, a Darwin, a Galileo, a Fulton or an Emerson, was subjected to ridicule or persecution; so that this objection should receive no serious consideration; but, on the contrary, we should carefully consider every fact which is brought to our attention; by doing this we will more readily ascertain the law upon which it is based.

In creating a Mental Image or an Ideal, we are projecting a thought into the Universal Substance (The Whole) from which all things are created. This means that recognition of Universal Substance brings about realization and a connection. When this tremendous fact begins to permeate your consciousness, when you really come into a realization of the fact that you (not your body, but the Ego), the "I," the spirit which thinks is an integral part of the great whole, that it is the same in substance, in quality, in kind, that the Creator could create nothing different from Himself, you will also be able to say, "The Father and I are one" and you will come into an understanding of the beauty, the grandeur, & the transcendental opportunities which have been placed at your disposal.

Exercise: Make use of the principle, recognize the fact that you are a part of the whole, and that a part must be the same in kind and quality as the whole; the only difference there can possibly by, is in degree. If connected and in tune, then your thoughts are mind are in fact heard and received by Creation.

14. Thought is a spiritual activity and is therefore endowed with creative power. This does not mean that some thought is creative, but that all thought is creative. Mankind is part of all there is. Our mind is connected to our body and to Spirit. Each cell is born, reproduces itself, dies and is absorbed. The maintenance of health and life itself depends upon the constant regeneration of these cells.

This change or growth of thought or enhancement of your mental attitude will not only bring you the material things which are necessary for your highest and best welfare, but will bring health and harmonious conditions generally. Imagine over time that your body, organs, and cells being are being regenerated to perfection and the old cells being cast away. In the same way, your power to attract the best from the world may operate if you are harmonious in mind, constructive in word and deed, and into action.

Exercise: Concentrate on Harmony, and when I say concentrate, I mean all that the word implies; concentrate so deeply, so earnestly, that you will be conscious of nothing but harmony. Remember, we learn by doing. Reading these lessons will get you nowhere. It is in the practical application that the value consists.

15. Difficulties and obstacles, indicate that we are either refusing to let go of what we no longer need, or refusing to accept what we require. Haanel gives a scientific example of a tiny parasite that adapts and grows wings rather than dying. In this way, people always have the inclination to adapt, improve and innovate. The question is when and how? Unfortunately, many times we are taught the same harmful lesson over and over until we are forced to take risk and truly change. To truly change, we must alter mind and spirit with our thoughts. In order to possess vitality, thought must be impregnated with love. Love is a product of the emotions. Therefore, thought and constructive emotion such as: Love, Gratitude, Faith and even Hope will most certainly stimulate the forces of the universe to assist you in your journey. This leads to the inevitable conclusion that if we wish to express abundance in our lives, we can afford to think abundance only, and as words are only thoughts taking form, we must be especially careful to use nothing but constructive and harmonious language, which when finally crystallized into objective forms, will prove to our advantage. This wonderful power of clothing thoughts in the form of words is what differentiates man from the rest of the animal kingdom. Words are thoughts and are therefore an invisible and invincible power which will finally objectify themselves in the form they are given. Overall, we may use constructive thinking and speech to master our destiny. To overcome error thoughts, we may use a conscious realization of the fact that Truth invariably destroys error. We do not have to laboriously shovel the darkness out; all that is necessary is to turn on the light. The same principle applies to every form of negative thought.

Exercise: Concentrate on Insight; take your accustomed relaxed position and focus the thought on the fact that to have a knowledge of the creative power of thought does not mean to possess the art of thinking. Let the thought dwell on the fact that knowledge does not apply itself. Our actions are not governed by knowledge, but by custom, precedent and habit. i.e. (Mental and Physical). That the only way we can get ourselves to apply knowledge is by a determined conscious effort. Call to mind the fact that knowledge unused passes from the mind, that the value of the information is in the application of the principle; continue this line of thought until you gain sufficient insight to formulate a definite program for applying this principle to your own particular problem.

16. Wealth should then never be desired as an end, but simply as a means of accomplishing an end. Success is contingent upon a higher goal ideal than the mere accumulation of riches, and he who aspires to such success must formulate an ideal for which he is willing to strive. Therefore, the essence of what we will do with wealth must be codified into a purpose of mind and desire. Haanel poses this question to a multi-millionaire with a railroad empire.... "Did you actually vision to yourself the whole thing? I mean, did you, or could you, really close your eyes and see the tracks? And the trains running? And hear the whistles blowing? Did you go as far as that?" "Yes." "How clearly?" "Very clearly."

Visualization must, of course, be directed by the will; we are to visualize exactly what we want; we must be careful not to let the imagination run riot. Thought is the plastic material with which we build images of our growing conception of life. Use determines its existence. We can form our own mental images, through our own interior processes of thought regardless of the thoughts of others, regardless of exterior conditions, regardless of environment of every kind, and it is by the exercise of this power that we can control our own destiny, body, mind and soul. The result will depend upon the mental images from which it emanates; this will depend upon the depth of the impression, the predominance of the idea, the clarity of the vision, the boldness of the image.

Exercise: Try to bring yourself to a realization of the important fact that harmony and happiness are states of consciousness and do not depend upon the possession of things. Things are effects and come as a consequence of correct mental states. So that if we desire material possession of any kind our chief concern should be to acquire the mental attitude which will bring about the result desired. This mental attitude is brought about by a realization of our spiritual nature and our unity with the Universal Mind which is the substance of all things. This realization will bring about everything which is necessary for our complete enjoyment. This is scientific or correct thinking. When we succeed in bringing about this mental attitude it is comparatively easy to realize our desire as an already accomplished fact; when we can do this we shall have found the "Truth" which makes us "free" from every lack or limitation of any kind.

Haanel: "Scientific thinking is a recognition of the creative nature of spiritual energy and our ability to control it."

17. We are accustomed to look upon the Universe with a lens of five senses, and from these experiences our anthropomorphic conceptions originate, but true conceptions are only secured by spiritual insight. This insight requires a quickening of the vibrations of the Mind, and is only secured when the mind is continuously concentrated in a given direction. The subconscious mind may be aroused and brought into action in any direction and made to serve us for any purpose, by concentration. All mental discovery and attainment are the result of desire plus concentration; desire is the strongest mode of action; the more persistent the desire, the more authoritative the revelation. Desire added to concentration will wrench any secret from nature.

Vibration is the action of thought; it is vibration which reaches out and attracts the material necessary to construct and build. There is nothing mysterious concerning the power of thought; concentration simply implies that consciousness can be focalized to the point where it becomes identified with the object of its attention. Always concentrate on the ideal as an already existing fact; this is the life principle which goes forth and sets in motion those causes which guide, direct and bring about the necessary relation, which eventually manifest in form.

Exercise: Concentrate as nearly as possible in accordance with the method outlined in this lesson; let there be no conscious effort or activity associated with your purpose. Relax completely, avoid any thought of anxiety as to results. Remember that power comes through repose. Let the thought dwell upon your object, until it is completely identified with it, until you are conscious of nothing else. Lesson: If you wish to eliminate fear, concentrate on courage, if you wish to eliminate lack, concentrate on abundance, and if you wish to eliminate disease, concentrate on health.

Haanel: "Intuition usually comes in the Silence; great minds seek solitude frequently."

18. Thought is the invisible link by which the individual comes into communication with the Universal, the finite with the Infinite, the seen with the Unseen. Thought is the magic by which the human is transformed into a being who thinks and knows and feels and acts. Growth is conditioned on reciprocal action, and we find that on the mental plane like attracts like, that mental vibrations respond only to the extent of their vibratory harmony. It is clear, therefore, that thoughts of abundance and health will respond only to similar thoughts. The connecting link between the individual and the Universal is Thought, and Love and Inner Harmony (a powerful emotion and feeling) is what fuels thought into manifestation or cooperation from the universe.

Exercise: Concentrate upon your power to create; seek insight, perception; try to find a logical basis for the faith which is in you. Let the thought dwell on the fact that the physical man lives and moves and has his being in the sustainer of all organic life air, that he must breathe to live. Then let the thought rest on the fact that the spiritual man also lives and moves and has his being in a similar but subtler energy upon which he must depend for life, and that as in the physical world no life assumes form until after a seed is sown, and no higher fruit than that of the parent stock can be produced; so in the spiritual world no effect can be produced until the seed is sown and the fruit will depend upon the nature of the seed, so that the results which you secure depend upon your perception of law in the mighty domain of causation, the highest evolution of human consciousness.

19. In the Moral World we find the same law; we speak of good and evil, but Good is a reality, something tangible, while Evil is found to be simply a negative condition, the absence of Good. We know that the ability of the individual to think in constructive ways is his ability to act upon the Universal Mind and convert it into dynamic mind, or mind in motion. We have then come to know that Mind is the only principle which is operative in the physical, mental, moral and spiritual world.

Exercise: Concentrate, and when I use the word concentrate, I mean all that the word implies; become so absorbed in the object of your thought that you are conscious of nothing else, and do this a few minutes every day. You take the necessary time to eat in order that the body may be nourished, why not take the time to assimilate your mental food? Let the thought rest on the fact that appearances are deceptive. The earth is not flat, neither is it stationary; the sky is not a dome, the sun does not move, the stars are not small specks of light, and matter which was once supposed to be fixed has been found to be in a state of perpetual flux. Try to realize that the day is fast approaching -- its dawn is now at hand -- when modes of thought and action must be adjusted to rapidly increasing knowledge of the operation of eternal principles.

20. God is Spirit. Spirit is the Creative Principle of the Universe. Man is made in the image and likeness of God. Man is therefore a spiritual being. The only activity which spirit possesses is the power to think. Thinking is therefore a creative process. All form is therefore the result of the thinking process. When you begin to perceive that the essence of the Universal is within yourself -- is you -- you begin to do things; you begin to feel your power; it is the fuel which fires the imagination; which lights the torch of inspiration; which gives vitality to thought; which enables you to connect with all the invisible forces of the Universe. It is this power which will enable you to plan fearlessly, to execute masterfully. This "breath of life" is a superconscious reality. It is the essence of the "I am." It is pure "Being" or Universal Substance, and our conscious unity with it enables us to localize it, and thus exercise the powers of this creative energy. Thought which is in harmony with the Universal Mind will result in corresponding conditions. Thought which is destructive or discordant will produce corresponding results. You may use thought constructively or destructively, but the immutable law will not allow you to plant a thought of one kind and reap the fruit of another.

You may have all the wealth in the world, but unless you recognize it and make use of it, it will have no value; so with your spiritual wealth: unless you recognize it and use it, it will have no value.

Lesson: Inspiration is from within. The Silence is necessary, the senses must be stilled, the muscles relaxed, repose cultivated. When you have thus come into possession of a sense of poise and power you will be ready to receive the information or inspiration or wisdom which may be necessary for the development of your purpose.

Exercise: Go into the Silence and concentrate on the fact that "In him we live and move and have our being" is literally and scientifically exact! That you ARE because He IS, that if He is Omnipresent He must be in you. That if He is all in all you must be in Him! That He is Spirit and you are made in "His image and likeness" and that the only difference between His spirit and your spirit is one of degree, that a part must be the same in kind and quality as the whole. When you can realize this clearly you will have found the secret of the creative power of thought, you will have found the origin of both good and evil, you will have found the secret of the wonderful power of concentration, you will have found the key to the solution of every problem whether physical, financial, or environmental.

21. "A Master-Mind thinks big thoughts. The creative energies of mind find no more difficulty in handling large situations, than small ones." Everything which we hold in our consciousness for any length of time becomes impressed upon our subconscious and so becomes a pattern which the creative energy will wave into our life and environment. This is the secret of the wonderful power of prayer The real secret of power is consciousness of power. The Universal Mind is unconditional; therefore, the more conscious we become of our unity with this mind, the less conscious we shall become of conditions and limitations, and as we become emancipated or freed from conditions we come into a realization of the unconditional. We have become free! Thus, prayer, meditation, and focused thought can be extremely effective in reaching your heights.

It is no easy matter to change the mental attitude, but by persistent effort it may be accomplished. The mental attitude is patterned after the mental pictures which have been photographed on the brain. If you do not like the pictures, destroy the negatives and create new pictures; this is the art of visualization. The Divine Mind makes no exceptions to favor any individual; but when the individual understands and realizes his Unity with the Universal principle he will appear to be favored because he will have found the source of all health, all wealth, and all power.

Exercise: Concentrate on the Truth. Try to realize that the Truth shall make you free, that is, nothing can permanently stand in the way of your perfect success when you learn to apply the scientifically correct thought methods and principles. Realize that you are externalizing in your environment your inherent soul potencies. Realize that the Silence offers an ever-available and almost unlimited opportunity for awakening the highest conception of Truth. Try to comprehend that Omnipotence itself is absolute silence, all else is change, activity, limitation. Silent thought concentration is therefore the true method of reaching, awakening, and then expressing the wonderful potential power of the world within.

22. Thoughts are spiritual seeds, which, when planted in the subconscious mind, have a tendency to sprout and grow, but unfortunately the fruit is frequently not to our liking. To remain healthy and regain health, we must increase the inflow and distribution of vital energy throughout the system, and this can only be done by eliminating thoughts of fear, worry, care, anxiety, jealousy, hatred, and every other destructive thought, which tend to tear down and destroy optimal health. It is through the law of vibration that the mind exercises this control over the body. We know that every mental action is a vibration, and we know that all form is simply a mode of motion, a rate of vibration. Therefore, any given vibration immediately modifies every atom in the body, every life cell is affected and an entire chemical change is made in every group of life cells. Through cooperation with our body, cell life and regeneration can be maintained at its highest levels.

Exercise: Concentrate on Tennyson's beautiful lines "Speak to Him, thou, for He hears, and spirit with spirit can meet, Closer is He than breathing, and nearer than hands and feet." Then try to realize that when you do "Speak to Him" you are in touch with Omnipotence. This realization and recognition of this Omnipresent power will quickly destroy any and every form of sickness or suffering and substitute harmony and perfection. Of course we should see a doctor if they can remove an infection and fix a problem. Thus, we should cooperate with all those available who should help us in a truthful manner while also cooperating with our bodies and spirit to heal, regenerate, and reach abundance. You will then more readily appreciate the ideal man, the man made in the image and likeness of God, and you will more readily appreciate the all originating Mind that forms, upholds, sustains, originates, and creates all there is.

23. One of the highest laws of success is service. Service to yourself and to humanity. It is inevitable that the entertainment of positive, constructive and unselfish thoughts should have a far-reaching effect for good. Compensation is the keynote of the universe. Nature is constantly seeking to strike an equilibrium. Where something is sent out something must be received; else there should be a vacuum formed.

You can make a money magnet of yourself, but to do so you must first consider how you can make money for other people. We make money by making friends, and we enlarge our circle of friends by making money for them, by helping them, by being of service to them. The first law of success then is service, and this in turn is built on integrity and justice. Keep in mind, generous thoughts filled with strength and vitality. Giving without expectation will form a vacuum which must be filled. Therefore, the laws of cause and effect will favor you with your sincere assistance and service to others.

Helping Others Mentally: If you desire to help someone, to destroy some form of lack, limitation or error, the correct method is not to think of the person whom you wish to help; the intention to help them is entirely sufficient, as this puts you in mental touch with the person. Then drive out of your own mind any belief of lack, limitation, disease, danger, difficulty or whatever the trouble might be. As soon as you have succeeded is doing this the result will have been accomplished, and the person will be free.

Attention develops concentration, and concentration develops Spiritual Power, and Spiritual Power is the mightiest force in existence. The power of attention is called concentration; this power is directed by the will; for this reason we must refuse to concentrate or think of anything except the things we desire. "Spirituality" is quite "practical," very "practical," intensely "practical." It teaches that Spirit is the Real Thing, the Whole Thing, and that Matter is but plastic stuff, which Spirit is able to create, mould, manipulate, and fashion to its will. Spirituality is the most "practical" thing in the world -- the only really and absolutely "practical" thing that there is!

Exercise: Concentrate on the fact that man is not a body with a spirit, but a spirit with a body, and that it is for this reason that his desires are incapable of any permanent satisfaction in anything not spiritual. Money is therefore of no value except to bring about the conditions which we desire, and these conditions are necessarily harmonious. Harmonious conditions necessitate sufficient supply, so that if there appears to be any lack, we should realize that the idea or soul of money is service, and as this thought takes form, channels of supply will be opened, and you will have the satisfaction of knowing that spiritual methods are entirely practical.

24. If you have practiced each of the exercises a few minutes every day, as suggested, you will have found that you can get out of life exactly what you wish by first putting into life that which you wish. Every form of concentration, forming Mental Images, Constructive Argument, and Autosuggestion are all simply methods by which you are enabled to realize the Truth.

When you master these steps, you will have mastered TRUTH. The method for removing this error is to go into the Silence and know the Truth; as all mind is one mind, you can do this for yourself or anyone else. If you have learned to form mental images of the conditions desired, this will be the easiest and quickest way to secure results; if not, results can be accomplished by argument, by the process of convincing yourself absolutely of the truth of your statement.

The absolute truth is that the "I" is perfect and complete; the real "I" is spiritual and can therefore never be less than perfect; it can never have any lack, limitation, or disease. The flash of genius does not have origin in the molecular motion of the brain; it is inspired by the ego, the spiritual "I" which is one with the Universal Mind, and it is our ability to recognize this Unity which is the cause of all inspiration, all genius.

Most people understand this word "GOD" to mean something outside of themselves; while exactly the contrary is the fact. It is our very life. Without it we would be dead. We would cease to exist. The minute the spirit leaves the body, our bodies are as nothing. Therefore, spirit is really, all there is of us. When the truth of this statement is realized, understood, and appreciated, you will have come into possession of the <u>Master-Key</u>.

Now, the only activity which the spirit possesses is the power to think. Therefore, thought must be creative, because spirit is creative. This creative power is impersonal and your ability to think is your ability to control it and make use of it for the benefit of yourself and others. The conditions with which you meet in the world without are invariably the result of the conditions obtaining in the world within, therefore it follows with scientific accuracy that by holding the perfect ideal in mind you can bring about ideal conditions in your environment. What is meant by thinking? Clear, decisive, calm, deliberate, sustained thought with a definite end in view. What will be the result? You will also be able to say, "It is not I that doeth the works, but the 'Father' that dwelleth within me, He doeth the works." You will come to know that the "Father" is the Universal Mind and that He does really and truly dwell within you, in other words, you will come to know that the wonderful promises made in the Bible are fact, not fiction, and can be demonstrated by anyone having sufficient understanding.

Codified, Revised and Extracted from the Master Key System by Dr. Haanel. Revisions by Prof. Mentz.

A SUMMARY OF THE SCIENCE OF THE GETTING RICH METAPHYSICS

There is a spiritual energy and force in every thought, from which all things are made, and which, in its original state, permeates, penetrates, and fills the interspaces of the Universe. A thought in this substance produces the thing that is imaged by the thought. Persons can form things in his their thought, and by impressing their thoughts upon formless substance (interspaces of the Universe) can cause the thing he they think about to be created. In order to do this, people must pass from the competitive to the creative mind. Otherwise they cannot be in harmony with formless intelligence, which is always creative and never competitive in Spirit.

People may come into full harmony with the formless substance by entertaining a lively and sincere gratitude for the blessings it bestows upon them. Gratitude unifies the mind of man with the intelligence of substance, so that man's thoughts are received by the formless. People can remain upon the creative plane only by uniting themselves with the formless intelligence through a deep and continuous feeling of gratitude. People must form a clear and definite mental image of the things they wish to have, to do, or to become, and they must hold this mental image in his their thoughts while being deeply grateful to the supreme that all his their desires are granted. People who wish to get rich must spend their leisure hours in contemplating their vision, and in earnest thanksgiving that the reality is being given to them.

Too much stress cannot be laid on the importance of frequent contemplation of the mental image, coupled with unwavering faith and devout gratitude. This is the process by which the impression is given to the formless and the creative forces set in motion. The creative energy works through the established channels of natural growth, and of the industrial and social order. All that is included in his mental image will surely be brought to people who follow the instructions given above, and whose faith does not waver. What they want will come to them through the ways of established trade and commerce.

In order to receive their own when it is ready to come to them, people must be in action in a way that causes them to more than fill their present place. They must keep in mind the purpose to get rich through realization of their mental image. And they must do, every day, all which can be done that day, taking care to do each act in a successful manner. They must give to every person a use value in excess of the cash value they receive, so that each transaction makes for more life, and they must hold the advancing thought so that the impression of increase will be communicated to all with whom they comes into contact.
The men and women who practice the foregoing instructions will certainly get rich, and the riches they receive will be in exact proportion to the definiteness of their vision, the fixity of their purpose, the steadiness of their faith, and the depth of their gratitude. *Wallace D. Wattles (1910) – Enhanced by Prof. Mentz

Wallace D. Wattles (1860-1911)

Wattles was an American author and success writer. His most famous work was *The Science of Getting Rich*, or otherwise known as: *Financial Success Through Creative Thought*. He did profess to study thinkers such as Descartes, Spinoza, Leibnitz, Schopenhauer, Hegel, and Emerson. Wattles has positively affected millions with his books and philosophy of Mind Sciences or New Thought. His other books, including *The Science of Being Great*, have some excellent commentary and mind exercises for metaphysical wholeness and health.

Dr. Charles F. Haanel (1866-1949)

Haanel wrote the *Master Key System* in the early 1900s, which sold over two-hundred-thousand copies by 1933. It originally had twenty-four parts. The book is devoted to mind development and achieving your life's dreams using applied metaphysics. Charles F. Haanel was an American author, millionaire, entrepreneur, and businessman who belonged to several Freemason-related societies: the American Scientific League, The Author's League of America, The American Society of Psychical Research, the St. Louis Humane Society, and the St. Louis Chamber of Commerce. *The Master Key System* is one of the classic studies in self-improvement, mind sciences, New Thought, and higher consciousness.

OTHER AUTHORS OF IMMEDIATE INTEREST

Carnegie, D. (1994) *How to Win Friends and Influence People*, New York: Pocket Books.

Carlson, R. (2001) Don't Sweat the Small Stuff About Money: Hyperion - Previously published as, Don't Worry Make Money

Chopra, D. (1996) *The Seven Spiritual Laws of Success*, London: Bantam Press.

Collier, R. (1970) *Be Rich*, Oak Harbor, WA : Robert Collier Publishing, Inc

Covey, S. R. (1989) *The 7 Habits of Highly Effective People*, London: Simon & Schuster.

Dyer, W. (1993) *Real Magic: Creating Miracles in Everyday Life*, New York: HarperCollins.

Shakti Gawain (1979) *Creative Visualization*: Mill Valley:

Haanel, C. F. (2000) *The Master Key System*, Pennsylvania: Wilkes-Barre.

Hill, N. (1960) *Think and Grow Rich*, New York: Fawcett Crest.

Marden, O. S. (1997) *Pushing to the Front, or Success under Difficulties*, Vols 1 & 2, Santa Fe, CA: Sun Books.

Mentz, G. S. (2007) Masters of the Secrets PA: Xlibris Publishing. www.mastersofthesecrets.com

Murphy, J. (2002) *The Power of Your Subconscious Mind*, New York: Bantam Books

Ponder, C. (1962) *The Dynamic Laws of Prosperity*, Camarillo, CA: DeVorss & Co.

Roman & Packer (1988), *Creating Money*: Tiburon: Kramer,

Price, J. R. (1987) *The Abundance Book*, Carlsbad, CA: Hay House

Smiles, S. (2002) *Self-Help: With Illustrations of Character, Conduct, and Perseverance, Oxford, UK: Oxford University Press.*

Tracy, B. (1993) *Maximum Achievement: Strategies and Skills that Will Unlock Your Hidden Powers to Succeed*, New York: Fireside.

Thomas Troward, (1904) *The Edinburgh Lectures on Mental Science*

Wattles, W.D (1976) *Financial Success through the Power of Thought* [*The Science of Getting Rich*], Rochester, Vermont: Destiny Books. (Written originally around 1910)

Written and Edited by George S Mentz, JD, MBA, CWM

*Note: The basic foundations of these writings are derived and taken from the 1912 writings Charles Haanel (1866-1949) and Wallace Wattles. Prof. Mentz has expanded these principles into a 21st Century writing. The bonus section summary is an critique and analysis of the 1910 writings of Wallace Wattles (1860-1911).

Prof. Dr. George Mentz, JD, MBA, CWM ™

- **The first person in the United States to achieve "Quad Designation" Status as a Lawyer, MBA, licensed financial planner, and Certified Financial Consultant.**
- **Earned Juris Doctorate Degree, Earned Accredited MBA Degree and international law graduate certificate/diplomé.**
- **Mentz Training Featured and quoted in the Wall Street Journal ™, The Hindu National, The Financial Times Asia, The Arab Times, and El Norte Latin America.**
- **International Senior Wealth Management for a Wall Street Firm**
- **Faculty Advisor and Chief for the Original Tax and Estate Planning Law Review**
- **Elected to the Advisory Board of the Global Finance Forum and the World E-Commerce Forum and the ERISA Fiduciary Guild.**
- **Author of Several books on Wealth Management, Human Potential, Success, & Project Management**
- **Faculty Appointments and Graduate Executive Training Appointments for law schools, business schools, and Training Centers in: Miami, Denver, Hong Kong, Nassau, San Diego, Silicon Valley, Virginia, New Orleans, Dubai, New York, India, and more.**
- **Training offices in Singapore, Hong Kong, Dubai, Beijing, Kuwait, USA, West Indies, and more.**
- **Prof. Mentz has been a recognized professor and counsel for the Diamond Law School Graduate Program for several years**
- **Prof. Mentz has been awarded several honorary doctorates for his writings and research.**

For More Information, Go to: www.mastersofthesecrets.com